Habits
of the
Heart

You _____ *are about to find paths to success wide enough for family, friends and fun!*

Habits of the Heart

Simple Ideas for Taking Paths to Success Wide Enough for Family, Friends and Fun

Jeff Conley

Some names have been changed to protect privacy.

I dedicate this book to the educators
who care enough to make a difference
for the kids in their classrooms.
This book is for the three teachers
who taught me to fly...
Dr. R. J. Bicker, Shirley Fields and E. M. Jones

Acknowledgments

This book reflects ten years of studying the human spirit, and I never could have completed it without the contributions of a few special people in my life. But first, let me thank God for his hand of guidance and direction over the last ten years. I hope to fulfill his vision for my life in this work and in others to come.

My family has been there to support me every step of the way. To my wife, Terri, thank you sweetheart for enduring all the weird looks when you tell people what I do for a living. Thank you for loving me no matter what and for sticking with me for the last sixteen years. To my children, Kenda and Collin, I'm so proud of you and love you more than you will ever know. Thanks to Mom for my sense of humor and to Dad for allowing me to find my own way in the world.

Thanks to all audience members who have stayed behind after one of my appearances and shared their stories of hope, commitment and balance. To all those difference makers who have crossed my path and created a turning point in my life, I want to say thank you. And finally, I could not be the person I am today without the wisdom, love and encouragement given to me by Zig and Jean Ziglar, Michael Josephson and Rene Chehardy.

What a privilege it is to stand on the shoulders of these giants and make a difference for others.

Contents

Introduction

• •

Try not to become a man of success but rather a man of value.

—Albert Einstein

I hear cries from the hearts of business people everywhere I go. They seem to be calling for answers to two tough questions:

1. How can I find the freedom to pursue my dreams and still provide for my family?
2. Is there any way to renew myself after a hard day at work without losing time with my family?

....

You can have both a dream career and a family life full of love and stability. It is possible to find a full life and a fulfilling career. The key to balance, renewal and the sense of inner peace you are seeking is to learn how to renew yourself each day by building and sustaining a Wealthy Heart.

What is a Wealthy Heart?

A Wealthy Heart is about being who you genuinely and uniquely are—free from pretenses and open to positive change. A Wealthy Heart is the result of a way of life built on foundations that provide a lasting sense of purpose, significance and love. A Wealthy Heart leads you to seek success down paths that are personally fulfilling, and broad enough to allow the important people in your life to take the journey with you.

While some might call the idea of a Wealthy Heart new, it's really an age-old way of living that is regaining recognition and acceptance. More and more people are coming to the realization that success at work without success in life is ultimately empty and lacking in deep satisfaction. I believe it is possible to be successful both at work and at home if you understand that there are many paths that lead to success.

....

The Hungers of the Heart

You can find your own path, one that allows your family to be part of your life along the way. Finding your own path is important, for its absence creates haunting hungers deep inside your heart. I call them the Hungers of the Heart—those deep feelings of yearning that convince you that there is a subtle, guiding force that patiently calls you to discover your reason for being here.

The Hungers of the Heart goad us to be more than the biological result of our parents' union. They call us to recognize that while we are all part of the body called humanity, each of us, individually, has a unique function that serves to support the health of the whole. The Hungers of the Heart are the motivators that start us on the search to discover our uniqueness and use it to make a difference.

But more often than we'd care to admit, the duration and intensity of our work takes a toll on our energy that leaves us no spirit for our families or our search. Our dominant desire on these occasions is to fold into the potato position and become one with our sofas.

....

During such periods of intensity at work, we tend to adapt to the demands of our jobs to get the work done. No problem. Not yet. Hard work is a virtue—but constant overwork is a liability. While periods of intensity and occasional sacrifices are justifiable in the short term, a work culture that demands habitual sacrifice is detrimental to family happiness and personal well-being. Constant intensity drowns out the drive the Hungers of the Heart create.

Every job has periods of intensity: accountants with their tax deadlines, lawyers preparing for a trial, salespeople at the end of the month, marketers involved in a product launch, and others, cycle through brief periods of intensity at work that are understandable.

However, constant habitual intensity is an overwork model intentionally sustained by many companies to achieve better bottom-line performance, at the expense of workers.

I will go so far as to say that there are many companies that encourage a work culture to evolve in which family responsibilities and the search for individual uniqueness are seen as career-limiting liabilities. In this kind of company, the only way to the top is through career loyalty to the tune of sixty- to seventy-hour weeks and broken promises to yourself and your

....

family. No amount of business success is worth the death of your family life or your dreams.

The Habits of the Heart

The good news is you do have choices. There are alternatives to the despotic ambitions that often rule with destructive force. You can find your sense of balance, renewal and purpose if you are loyal to the concept of Habits of the Heart, a series of questions you can ask yourself, to quell the hungers and achieve a Wealthy Heart.

The story of Roy Neel illustrates the concept of rejection of self-imposed, slave-like work habits. Roy's story appeared in the March 6, 1995, issue of Newsweek, which described him as the deputy chief of staff in the Clinton administration, whose days were full, with workweeks of fifty-five hours, and always he was on call:

> "I got downright tired of being tethered to my beeper 24 hours a day," says Neel. A seemingly tame but wrenching episode with Walter, his nine-year-old son, convinced him that

work, even for the President of the United States, is not worth the price. Walter and his dad were heading out the door for a long-promised baseball game when the phone rang. It was the President. Little Walter was not impressed. When Neel looked up an hour later, Walter was gone. He had bummed a ride with a neighbor, leaving dad holding the phone. "Our society has become schizophrenic," says Neel. "We praise people who want to balance their lives, but reward those who work themselves to death."

Roy Neel listened to his wake-up call. He quit his powerful and influential position because he saw one of life's biggest red flags and paid attention to it. *When your work becomes the dominating force affecting your family, it's time to make a change—a change of attitude or a change of work.* Roy chose to take a lobbying job that would allow him to slow down at home and escape from his life that was out of control. What will your choice be when you hit the wall? My purpose with this book is to provide you with a road map of Habits of the Heart that will help you make choices that are right for your family.

....

The military has zero tolerance for errors. Their motto is, "We don't strive for excellence, we maintain it." That's a fairly high expectation for performance. But military personnel accept the challenge and succeed more often than not at meeting those expectations. Recently, my wife, Terri, and I took our kids on an educational vacation to Washington, D.C., and one of the highlights was Arlington National Cemetery.

As we walked through the cemetery we came upon the memorial amphitheater where ceremonies are held to honor those who have made the greatest sacrifice for our freedom. As we entered and walked to the stage area, I noticed an inscription above the arch of the platform. It read, "When we assumed the soldier, we did not lay aside the citizen." I remember thinking, "Wow, the military doesn't think of soldiers as killing machines who destroy on command. They realize that their soldiers are sons, daughters, husbands, wives, friends, citizens and well-trained professionals who protect our freedom and liberty as Americans." I was proud to explain that inscription to my children.

But I must say, after ten years of working with more than five hundred different companies on the corporate battleground, that kind of a sense of pride is hard to come by in the business world. Far too many

....

companies are operating with a take-no-prisoners culture and the casualties are mounting. While the bottom line may pass inspection, too often the costs of increased business are marriages that suffer from habitual neglect, children who long for a deeper relationship with their parents, and a desperately unhappy work force that seems to succeed at work but fails at family, friendship, faith and fun.

If you are a business leader, I hope that you will be open to the two messages this book presents. At the corporate level, the message is: *Build people first and people will build a company that lasts.* Practice the habit of people first. I've seen the remarkable difference this long-term strategy can make, as opposed to the short-term approach of profits over people. At the personal level, the message is: *Success without lasting love is empty.*

This book is written for people like my friend Jack, an entrepreneur. His success has been celebrated often in the business section of our local paper, but he is hurting in a way money can't heal. He's divorced his third wife, supports kids from different spouses in several states, and never thinks he has the time to be the dad he says he wants to be. He traded his dreams of success for his family. You don't have to do that.

I'm also thinking of Bob, a good client who is the CEO of an insurance firm and a supporter of the arts in his community. By his own admission, he told me that he was so addicted to the adrenaline rush of business that he often came home late during the years his kids were little. Today, Bob's son lives out of the country and won't return his dad's e-mail or phone calls. Bob told me he'd give almost everything to have his son back in his life.

This book is to provide comfort and direction for the thousands of other top performers I've met who are making it at work but are frustrated with their lives. Many have expressed to me feelings of guilt about their successes, because they were expending so much energy and time at the office they often had nothing left for the most important people in their world—their family. Far too many of us, myself included, have tried to make a name for ourselves, prove our self worth or pursue wealth without letting our families into our lives.

Stephen and Marie were an entrepreneurial-minded husband and wife team. For twenty years, they threw themselves into their business. She ran the daily operations and he was the visionary and the motivator.

They grew their garage start-up to almost one billion dollars in revenue. Often on the road apart from each other, or arriving home late after entertaining clients, they had as good a marriage as you can manage under such pressing circumstances, but rarely did they see each other and they never took any time off. Marie suddenly died of a heart attack in her mid-forties. I don't have to tell you Stephen would start all over with nothing if he could get Marie back. Life doesn't always happen as planned.

Vickie's story is one to take to heart. I met Vickie while speaking at her company's annual sales meeting. Vickie was a perennial leader in business volume and admired by her peers. From the outside, you would never know how much of a heartache Vickie had. But she was miserable. After I had shared the information that you are about to read, Vickie came up to me in tears thanking me for reminding her that she can always get another piece of business or another job but her kids can't get another mom.

This book is not about compromising your dreams for the sake of your family. This book is about developing the confidence and the freedom and the Wealthy Heart to say, "No" to some paths of success, so you can say, "Yes" to other paths of success—paths that are

....

broad enough to allow your family to take the journey with you.

The Habits of the Heart that I will share with you are a road map of how to make the journey to career vitality while holding hands with family, friendship, faith and fun. It's time to give our families all they deserve instead of giving them everything but ourselves. Is it worth it? I think it is.

→   ←

Zig Ziglar has been my mentor. My wife, Terri, and I both went to work for him during the '80s, helping to promote his seminars. I can honestly say our lives were changed from the first day we met him in Dallas, Texas. The opportunities I have today as a professional speaker developed when Zig helped me publish my first work in 1992. Zig was a big believer in giving people a Checkup from the Neck Up and trying to identify Hardening of the Attitudes. In keeping with Zig's approach, I've developed a questionnaire for self-assessment that I call The Wealthy Heart Checklist. Rate yourself and your present quality of life using the following twenty-three items. *Score each item on a scale of one to ten* in which the lower numbers mean you strongly disagree with the statement on the left and the higher numbers mean you agree with it. Upon completion, compare your score with the comments at the end.

The Wealthy Heart Checklist

My children feel I'm involved in their lives.   ___
I'm making a good living and have a full life.   ___
I love what I do for a living.   ___
I'm pleased with the level of support from
    my friends.   ___
I'm pleased with the amount of time I have
    to spend with my family.   ___
I'm pleased with my level of involvement
    in my children's lives   ___
I know my kids' best friends.   ___
My kids' teachers know who I am.   ___
My spouse and I are intimate as friends.   ___
I have enough time to do the things
    I want to do away from work.   ___
I have a lot of fun at work.   ___
During a day off, I can rest without
    being restless.   ___
I feel a sense of purpose in my life.   ___
I take time to think proactively each day.   ___

....

I usually laugh out loud every day.   ___
I'm pleased with my progress toward
    achieving my goals in life.   ___
I feel my spiritual life is complete.   ___
I feel that what I do makes a difference at work.___
I feel as though I have time to enjoy life.   ___
I am happy.   ___
I'm confident enough to say no to some
    work-related activities that threaten the
    stability of my family.   ___
I keep all my commitments at work
    and at home.   ___
I know what makes my spouse feel loved.   ___

Tally your total score.   ___

If you scored:

230–184   Congratulations, you have found the
Habits of the Heart and put them to work in your life.
You should have quite a sense of accomplishment about
what you've done. Way to go!

184–86   Reveille is blowing, alarm clocks are
ringing and this is your wake-up call. Go back and

....

highlight all of the items you ranked at 7 or below. If you have fewer than six items identified, you're very close to having a Wealthy Heart. If you have more than six items, you're in the right place to make some lasting changes to create the life you want by learning to practice the Habits of the Heart.

85–23 You feel trapped. Don't give up. The Hungers of the Heart that haunt you can be fed in a way that can lead you to success in life, in love and at work. The Habits of the Heart offer hope and a road map enabling you to find your Wealthy Heart. Let's go to work and put things back together again with some immediate ways of thinking differently about your life, your family and your career.

Confessions of a Working Warrior

• •

I do dimly perceive that whilst everything around me is ever changing, underlying all that changing is a living power that is changeless, that holds all together.

—Mahatma Gandhi

"I love what I do but I think I could be a lot happier if I did a little less of it. I'm overwhelmed by the constant crisis mentality at work but can't talk about it. I can work sixty hours a week, then seventy or eighty and it doesn't seem to matter. One day just fades into the next and there's no time to do what I want to do.

••

"Oh, don't get me wrong, there are rewards and I celebrate when a project succeeds. But then I feel curiously empty when the adrenaline rush and the pressures to perform are gone. I can't seem to relax or rest without being restless. I know I want to throttle back a bit but it's as if I don't know who I am if I'm not running ninety miles per hour on some quest.

"Is there any way to keep my edge at work but also slow down and brake some of this intensity in my life? We're doing okay financially, but personally, well that's another story. My marriage is in trouble and I know flight attendants better than I know my kids. This is not what I thought I was working toward. What happened?"

Anchor Your Thinking

The above comments are collective cries of the heart from hundreds of people I've worked with over the years. Their perspectives have helped me determine what developing a Wealthy Heart is. A person who has a Wealthy Heart lives a philosophy that states, *I can respond best to the demands of uncertainty by anchoring my thinking in a base of changeless values.* A Wealthy Heart becomes the anchor of your authenticity

••

and helps you weather the storms of endless pressure and uncertainty.

The *first step* toward building a Wealthy Heart is to recognize that it is impossible for a human being to keep up with the relentless pace of technology. You and I both know that microprocessors will never reach a point where the marketplace will say, "OK, I guess two thousand megahertz is fast enough for everyone." It's reasonable to assume that the thirst for speed will never be quenched.

Yet, we remain naïve and strangely determined to keep up as best we can. We throw ourselves into our work. It's exciting! We're on the cutting edge of life in the business world and a few successes along the way seem to build a sense of assurance. Consequently, so much of our time and energy are spent at work that we tend to develop a work-centered image of ourselves.

Professional Identity

I call this work-centered image the Professional Identity. The *second step* toward building and sustaining a Wealthy Heart is to control your professional identity. Here's an example from my world. For ten years, I've traveled the country giving motivational speeches at business conferences and conventions.

....

Performing at sixty of these corporate events every year and getting many standing ovations in the process, I began to think of myself as the greatest professional speaker who ever lived—"I'm Speakerman!"

In my mind, Speakerman had all the answers to the puzzles of life. He was this larger-than-life character who flew all over America speaking to audiences, with but one objective in mind: to save every human being in his path. Speakerman was always a hit, dazzling audiences with his heartfelt messages of hope. But I soon learned that too much of a good thing isn't healthy.

I started thinking of myself as Speakerman in everything I did. Speakerman mingles with the commoners at his son's soccer game. "That's my boy who just scored that goal...He's SPEAKERBOY!" It was Speakerman's daughter who played on her sixth-grade championship basketball team..."SPEAKER-GIRL scores!" At the grocery store, at church and even at home I was Speakerman and only Speakerman. I was feeling great about myself, and totally oblivious to how difficult I had become to live with.

Whenever I did particularly well with an audience, I would always run to the phone and call my kids. Mind you, I did this for one reason. I wanted them to know how great their father was at what he did for a living. Every time I'd call, I'd go on and on about how great things went. I did this and then I did that, me, me, me, me, me. I did this because I desperately wanted to hear my children say, "Ohhh Fatherrr, we have been born unto such a super-achieving human being. How blessed we must be. Oh thank you Fatherrr!"

Was I sick or what? I later began to understand that what I was actually doing was seeking validation as a father through what I was doing for a living. My entire image of myself was centered around Speakerman, my Professional Identity.

Terri, bless her heart, did her best to snap me back into the real world. After one trip when Speakerman was high on having done particularly well, she gave me a much-needed dose of reality. She said, "You've got a real important job don't you."

"Oh yes baby I do. You have no idea how vital my job is to the success of America."

Terri educated me with astonishing skill when she replied, "We know things are demanding at work. That's the reason we keep things real simple for you around the house. At home, your only job is to take out the trash and, I hear the truck coming now, big boy, you'd better run!" I remember thinking…"Hmmm, Speakerman's only job at home is picking up trash? Maybe Speakerman isn't important at home. Duh ya think?"

I got the message. Speakerman is important at work, but until he can learn to control himself around the house, my family doesn't want him around. I had to learn to leave Speakerman on the plane, at the office or in the car but don't bring him home. When I'm at home, my family wants: a caring husband…a lover…a friend…a daddy…a bedtime reader…a listener…a cheerleader…a dog walker (always carry a bag for the puppy's business)…a homework helper…an intimidator for annoying telemarketers…a carpool driver…a shoulder to cry on…a handyman…and another responsible life partner to co-manage the demands of raising a family.

By thinking of myself only as Speakerman, I was guilty of being emotionally absent in all my other identities and it was building a wall between me and my family. A Wealthy Heart knows that our identity is shaped by who we are, not by what we do. I had allowed my professional identity, just one aspect of who I am, to become a counterfeit representation of who I am in total.

Has anything like this ever happened to you? If you are married with children, and you are the Regional Vice President of a company making microprocessors

. . . .

for PCs, have you ever come home as—Chip Man? If you are the CEO of a soft drink distribution company, have you ever come home to your family after a hard day still thinking of yourself as—Coke Queen?

You don't have to make that mistake ever again. We are so much more than our professional identity. I didn't realize this until one day when I came home from a week-long business trip and my two kids rushed up to me as I came through the door. They looked up at me and yelled out a single word that changed my life. They said, "Daddy!" Prior to this event, I never saw myself as Daddy. I was too busy being…SPEAKERMAN!

I was so busy being Speakerman, I never thought of myself as Daddy. Whenever I thought of Daddy, I had a competing image of my daddy, Noel Conley. The image was of him as a thirty-five-year-old man and me as a ten-year-old. We're playing catch in the back yard. Dad was the coach of the Little League team and he was teaching me the finer points of right field (because that's where you put fat kids who can't throw).

When I heard my kids yell out "Daddy," and suddenly I knew they meant me, it changed my life. For the first time, I began to understand that I will ALWAYS be a father, a son, a husband, a friend, a neighbor, a citizen, a brother and a child of God even if there are

....

times when Speakerman fails. These changeless foundations of life began to give me strength to compete and keep up with a techno-centric world. I was learning how to build a Wealthy Heart.

Think of all the roles you have in life. Only one of those roles is work related. Remember, I over-inflated the importance of my professional identity to the point that it overshadowed the other vital roles in my life: those of being a successful husband, father, friend, neighbor, citizen, son, brother and child of God.

I realized that true joy and lasting happiness aren't found in your professional identity alone, but in a mixture of vitality in all of these areas. Interestingly enough, I found that once I had a Wealthy Heart no work-related setback could defeat me. The beauty of achieving a Wealthy Heart is that it is permanent. I have found that if:

- my wife and I have a marriage of total trust;
- my faith is unwavering;
- my children know I love them no matter what;
- I'm competent in my work related skills; and
- I have rich friendships based on mutual support,

I can weather the storms of downsizing, forced early outs or sudden self-employment, as well as any temporary downturn in my business. The industrial-strength WOW! is that a Wealthy Heart built on trust-worthy relationships with my God, my spouse, my children and my friends sustains me no matter what happens to me professionally.

There is a time and place for Speakerman, but there is also a time and a place for our other life roles. A Wealthy Heart has the wisdom to control our Professional Identity and to match all of our needed roles with the appropriate times, places and situations.

One-Line Summaries

- Set boundaries during periods of intensity at work in order to come home whole at the end of the battle.
- No one can *stay* on the cutting edge.
- Develop a Wealthy Heart based on a foundation of your changeless values, which function as anchors during the storms of life.
- Don't let your Professional Identity overpower the other roles of life.
- There is a place for Speakerman. But that place is not at home.

The Hungers of the Heart

●●●●●●●●●●●●●●●●●●●●●●●●●●●●●●●●

If the foundation is not exactly right, no win at the top will be able to fill the cracks at the bottom.

—Stephen Arterburn

Over the years, I've made a discovery. The people who seem to be the happiest in life and the most fulfilled all share one thing in common. It's not riches, talent, intelligence or beauty. What the happiest and most fulfilled people seem to share is the learned ability to feed the Hungers of the Heart.

....

What are the Hungers of the Heart?

There are six Hungers of the Heart. They are the intensely powerful and intuitive feelings that simultaneously push, or drive, you toward your ambitions and pull, or call, you to your highest potential. These feelings of drive and calling work together to bring about a natural harmony and rhythm to life. Feeding these Hungers of the Heart makes us fully mature people who can be both result-oriented at our work and more connected and loving in our relationships.

The three hungers of *the drive* are the easiest to recognize. The drive is the force that makes you want to provide for your family and leads you to achieve, and to excel at whatever target goal you focus on. These feelings are the ones that fuel your competitive fires, give you your ambition, and point you toward others who can help you succeed at work. However, if you only feed the hungers of drivenness, you may achieve but you will soon grow tired of achieving for achievement's sake. After regular trips to the winner's circle, we begin to ask, "Is this all there is? Is my life always going to be about achieving a series of goals? Goals are good but

···

the feelings of achievement don't last." No there's a lot more to life than goals.

To restore your sense of harmony, you must give equal attention to all the hungers that fuel your drive *and* all those that fuel your calling. Listening to both the drive and the call will give you a sense of direction and purpose.

The three hungers of calling are those that compel you to search for a sense of lasting value in life. Begin to ask questions of yourself regarding lasting love, inner peace and what you'll be remembered for. The answers to these questions can't be found at the office. They can only be found when you open ourself to feeding the calling hungers as well as the driving hungers. Once you learn to feed all the hungers, you can achieve balance in your life. By understanding how to maintain *balance* we bring a sense of meaning and significance, and a sense of purpose to our lives.

There are two broad categories—the drive and the call—that contain the six Hungers of the Heart. These three driving hungers are:

- The *drive to succeed* at work doing something you love to do…

....

Succeeding is intoxicating, especially if your success comes in a field of work that is enjoyable to you. But winning at work alone without winning at life can have significant negative side effects. I want to succeed at work. But I also want to succeed at home, in my faith, and with my friends and I want some sense of meaning in my life. If you lose these other things in the pursuit of what you want you will never be truly successful. Succeeding at work usually comes first. But don't fall into the trap that tells you the holes in your heart can be filled by more achievement at work. We must learn to feed those hungers in other ways.

• The *drive to make a difference* for others…

What a gratifying feeling of joy it is to make a difference in the life of another human being. I know a lot of pastors and corporate executives who believe strongly in service to others. As noble as this is, there is still the need to understand that if you are one who focuses on being a difference maker for others, first make sure you don't lose your family from neglect while you are out saving the world. Make sure you make regular deposits of love and attention at home that always stay ahead of your withdrawals by absence.

- The *drive to be attracting* to others...

    Being attracting means influencing others by developing the qualities within yourself that draw people to you. Your sense of integrity, your spirit of service, the desire to build unity, your passion, tenacity, openness and sense of humor all serve as magnetic attributes that create a desire within other people to want to be around you. Cultivate these qualities at home and with your friends, as well as at work, and the relationships in your life will be richer and more rewarding.

These driving hungers are overwhelming in power and can bring about initial positive changes. But here's a word of caution. Without the counterweight of the calling hungers, the driving hungers can take ordinary well-intentioned people and consume them in a pattern of more is better, ultimately leading them down the path to becoming emotionally immature, "me first," acquisition-driven workaholics. Those who are driven without

• •

the balance of the call tend to be candidates for high-maintenance relationships and may find themselves successful in only one aspect of life (work) and desperately unhappy with life as a whole.

The three calling Hungers of the Heart are:

• The *call to discover your unique purpose* for this world...

In the beginning of your life, you follow the direction of others and complete tasks they set out for you to do. But you want your own sense of control and soon learn to move beyond the externally driven tasks to an internally driven desire for goals. Your goals lead you to achieve but you soon you find that the setting and achieving of goals time after time, while rewarding, proves to lack a lasting sense of meaning. Then one day, you hear a faint whisper calling you to follow a new path. Following that call and learning along the way is what gives us our sense of purpose. All of us have a uniquely designed sense of purpose, and the journey to feed that hunger without neglecting the other hungers is what this book is all about.

- The *call to love and be loved* for a lifetime…

What would lasting love mean to you? I mean the kind of unconditional love that will always be there affirming you and giving you the strength to believe in yourself? What does it mean to really love another person for life? Can you love in your heart without demonstrating that love in action? Do you allow other people to demonstrate love to you, without deflecting their gift of love because of your feelings of betrayal or abandonment from the past?

Love, like life, is confusing. It means a lot of different things to a lot of people. For our purposes, the word love means the habit of showing a visible love, the habit of doing things for others in the way they want them done. Today it's not enough just to say, "I love you." We must say it, and more importantly, give those we love reasons to believe our words.

- The *call to discover your sense of lasting inner peace*…

Inner peace is not a macho-less term. It takes strength to admit your weaknesses and find

....

inner peace. It requires understanding what humility is.

Bum Phillips was a coach in the National Football League years ago and Bum had a way of instilling a sense of humility in his players when they got a little too cocky after a big win. Bum would always remind them, "No matter how great you prove yourselves to be on the football field, always remember that the attendance at your funeral will be dependent upon the weather."

Humility, inner peace and achievement are not mutually exclusive. You can actually find yourself able to achieve things you never thought you could if you understand that worth and your sense of inner peace don't come from what you accomplish. They come from recognizing the lasting value of forever being a child of God.

All of the hungers must be fed. Recurring problems tend to happen when only one or two of the six hungers are recognized, selected and cared for. The others become neglected consciously or unconsciously and it is this neglect that causes so much damage to our sense of balance, inner peace and happiness. *Every human being is driven and called by the Hungers of the Heart.* The struggle is to understand the value of feeding them all, as opposed to just a few.

Companies tend to develop problems when they unconsciously starve these hungers. Many of today's workplaces view people simply as units of productivity. When that happens, a work culture of constant intensity tends to evolve and people emotionally withdraw from each other because they are not encouraged to feed their Hungers of the Heart.

Emotional withdrawal is poisonous at work because it keeps project team members from trusting one another. Allowed to grow unrestricted, this emotional withdrawal can result in people coming to see work as an empty exchange of output for money. In these situations, business leaders get compliance from their people but not commitment.

However, when people are encouraged to develop the habits of feeding all six hungers, they master the drive and the call, which in turn leads to success in all major life roles. You get better employees, better parents, better spouses, better neighbors, better friends and better citizens—a true social and business win/win.

....

Think about it. What good does it do to get elected to the Whatever-It-Is-You-Do Hall of Fame (via the drive) and feel inadequate, because you've reached the pinnacle of business success, but you've laid no foundation for lasting value (via the call). What if you lead a movement that brings about far-reaching and positive social change but your kids won't speak to you because while you were out saving the world, you weren't there for them? It takes both the drive and the call. It takes feeding all of the Hungers of the Heart to achieve a balance and rhythm of life. All the hungers are interconnected.

....

> **Balance, meaning, success and happiness are best achieved when all our Hungers of the Heart are regularly fed by the Habits of the Heart.**

The Hungers That Drive Us To Succeed

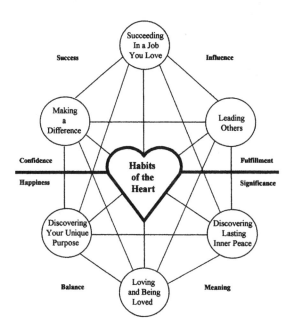

The Hungers That Call Us To Significance

The Habits of the Heart

● ●

For ten years I've wrestled with meeting the objective of finding a simple way to feed all the Hungers of the Heart every day and I believe God has given me a vision for how it can be done.

My quest began when I started asking myself some soul-searching questions. I wrote them down in my day planner: What's my purpose in life? What are my values? Am I confident enough in my values to protect them with decisions of integrity? Do my kids think I'm a good father? Does my wife think I'm a good husband? What are my strengths and how can I use them to help others?

....

These questions were important to me because *they challenged me to find a changeless sense of direction in times of constant change and uncertainty.*

They helped me to feel connected with a higher purpose and part of something that was bigger than myself. I didn't know at the time that these questions would have any value to anyone other than me. But over the years, many people from all walks of life have told me of the value they have found in asking themselves similar questions.

I began working to compile and condense my notes into a list of shorter questions relating to my quest. I named those bite-sized questions Habits of the Heart.

Each Habit-of-the-Heart question is meant to be a gentle reminder of the feedings necessary to achieve a Wealthy Heart lifestyle. I hope that you will be as richly rewarded as I have been, just by asking these simple questions every day:

- Am I sure about what matters most?
- Did I make a difference today?
- Am I secure in who I am regardless of my performance?
- Did I schedule some quiet time today?

....

- What did I do to show my family that I love them?
- Did I keep all my commitments (especially those at home)?
- Did I protect my honesty and integrity?
- Did I read or learn anything new?
- Was I kind to someone else without expecting anything in return?
- Did I laugh today?
- Was I a model of excellence at work today?
- If today was a day off, did I rest or was I restless?
- Did I provide emotional support for my family today?
- What will I do differently tomorrow?

Asking yourself …

Am I sure about what matters most?

feeds the Hungers of the Heart by developing the habit of …

Clarity

Am I Sure about What Matters Most?

● ●

Though client demands drive our days, we also have the flexibility and the freedom to make our own schedules and decide how and where to spend our time. Take advantage of that flexibility.

—J. Michael Cook, CEO, Deloitte & Touche

There is a new wave of organizational development under way in America in which leaders walk their co-workers through a process to discover their organization's core values. Then they hold each other accountable to live by those values and make decisions consis-

....

tent with them. This action plants the seeds of greatness within the hearts of all employees and equips everyone with the same barometer for ethical results. When the core values are written on hearts as well as on paper, and protected and used by decision makers, the company thrives and employees are happier, more supportive and more productive at work.

Just as this process works for organizations, it also works for individuals.

Are you sure about what matters most? Do you know your core values at the conscious level and are you prepared to use them as a decision-making tool to help direct your life and career?

Several years ago, I took the time to ask myself the question, "Am I sure what matters most?" The answer led me to develop my list of priorities, or core values. I wrote these values down and also prioritized them, in order to help me make better decisions about my career path and my family. Looking at the list, I found it easier to resist some opportunities that at the time seemed to be the only way to advance in my career. There are many paths to success and living by your core values helps you find the paths that most people overlook.

I got a phone call from a potential client who wanted to hire me to speak at his event in Palm Springs,

....

California. I asked for the date he had in mind and he told me it was March 27. I looked on my calendar and a fishing trip with my daughter was planned for the 27th, which was her Girl Scout troop's annual Daddies and Daughters Day.

I said, "I would love to come to Palm Springs to speak but I've got a conflict. Can we shift this speech to another day during the conference?"

"No, we're pretty locked in with this date," he said.

"By the way Jeff, where are you speaking on the 27th?"

"I'm not speaking," I said. "I'm taking Kenda on a fishing trip with her Girl Scout troop."

"Jeff, I tell you what we'll do. Let's give you the closing general session the afternoon of the 28th. I had someone else in mind but I think you'll do a better job."

"Oh, why is that?" I asked.

"We wanted someone to talk about balance and how every one can make a difference, but it's obvious you don't just talk about it, you live it."

I accepted the date and the compliment, then hung up the phone and began to cry. You see, not long before that I would have taken his offer of the 27th and gone home explaining to my daughter that business was calling me away and there was nothing I could do. I had to learn that I did have a choice. My thinking began to change when I took the time to understand what matters most to me.

I asked myself what are the most important things in my life? What is so important that I'd be willing to die for it? Obviously my family was on that list and work wasn't. Then I got a question in my heart that pierced my soul. If my family is important enough to die for, shouldn't they be important enough to live for? I had to learn that if I say my family is important but I don't do anything to protect our relationship then family has no real value, it just sounds good. I wanted to give my family what they deserved not just the leftovers.

I started making decisions that really did reflect how much I value my family, instead of just talking about it. I expected to take a few career hits over these decisions, but I found instead that people were more interested in how I was able to keep my sense of values so clear. I shared with them the idea of Habits of the Heart and they wanted a list of my questions for themselves.

One thing led to another and now I have a fulfilling career teaching others how to take different paths to success, paths that are wide enough so their families can make the journey with them.

••

It was Monday, the day after Father's Day, when I got a call from Max Martin. Max was a forty-three-year-old businessman whom I had met about one year earlier at his company's annual convention. Max had been honored as one of the company's top performers and was presented to his peers as a role model.

I met Max while speaking at his convention on the topic "Living Your Values…How to Walk Your Talk." During my speech, I asked the management professionals in the audience to define their core values by asking themselves, "What matters most?" I challenged them to not only define their values but also develop a life of personal integrity by walking their talk both at work and at home.

I encouraged them to make a list of their values and rank them in order of importance. I also challenged them to consult this list anytime they felt indecisive or confused. I told them that consciously knowing what matters most is the first step toward remaining effective in the face of relentless change and that is the key to maintaining a sense of balance in life.

Apparently, this message hit pretty close to home with Max because he waited patiently until everyone else had left the room and he came over to talk to me. I listened to his story of how he was working seven days

· ·

a week to keep up with demand. Max was a proud man and well respected by his peers, yet he felt he was short-changing his family and he didn't want to lose them but he didn't know what to do.

I asked him if he had ever discovered his core values and held himself accountable to live by those values. He said he had just listed and ranked his values during my speech. I asked if I could see his core values and he handed me his list. His number one value was honoring God. Number two was demonstrating how much he loved his family in the daily actions he takes. Number three was helping others and number four was excelling at work.

Max knew that his work schedule and his life choices weren't aligning with what he valued. He felt trapped, so we talked about how living a life that is inconsistent with your core values causes *stealthy stress,* the kind that really never appears on any radar screens until it's too late. I knew the next question I was to ask would be a tough one but I felt compelled to ask it for the sake of Max and his family. I asked if he felt he could maintain his integrity to his values and still keep up his current pace at work. Max looked down at the floor for a few seconds, then looked back up and courageously said, "No."

I complimented his honesty and encouraged him to go home and openly discuss these issues with his wife. I didn't hear from Max until the phone rang that Monday after Father's Day. "Jeff I did what you said. I went home and showed my wife what you and I had talked about and she totally supported me. We looked at all the alternatives and given our situation, we decided to lay out a plan for me to make a career change."

Max went on to say, "I began a search and found a company that would allow me more flexibility so I could be more involved at home. This last year has been a complete turnaround in terms of our quality of life. My marriage is better, my kids feel like I'm there for them and I've got to tell you, Jeff, yesterday was the first Father's Day in twelve years that I really felt like a dad. Thank you."

I believe there are millions of other Max Martins out there struggling with the same issues. You all know work is important, but there are other priorities in our lives that need your attention. Agreeing with me is easy. The question is—What are you prepared to do about it?

Asking yourself …

Did I make a difference today?

feeds the Hungers of the Heart by
developing the habit of …

Serving Others

Did I Make a Difference Today?

• •

In order to make a difference, you've got to make something change. Not only do you have to embrace change, you've got to elevate it, you've got to make things different. You need to become the kind of change agents that I call "difference makers." You need to be difference makers in our everyday business, and you need to be difference makers at home.

Most people are afraid of change because change creates uncertainty. If everything changes, you have chaos and it's easy to lose your bearing. You cannot positively direct change without a star to steer by. In times of change, you need some anchors that are unchangeable, which is where your core values come into play. Your ethical values become the solid foundation, the guiding star, the anchor points for change. Your ethical values, once they are alive in your heart, are the North Star that guides you during times of change.

Let's examine your values—your personal values and your business values. Michael Josephson, founder of the Josephson Institute of Ethics in Marina del Rey, California, defines values as "the ideas, the beliefs, the desires that shape your attitudes and motivate action." If you want your employees to behave a certain way, if you want them motivated to do a certain task, but your values and the values of your organization are inconsistent, it's not going to happen.

What are your operational values? Operational values are the ones that people actually work by. You'll find in many cases they're very different from the beautiful mission statement hanging on the boardroom wall.

Regardless of the mission statement you have tacked up in the lunchroom or tucked away in your file cabinet, you do not have the ability to make a difference unless your stated values and your mission statement live in the hearts of your people.

Anyone can sit down and write a mission statement, but the truly painful part of the process is

....

getting your people to live it. Four things have to happen in order for your mission statement and values to live in the hearts of your people.

1. Everyone must understand his or her impact in the organization.
2. Leaders must understand that they must model their values. Whether you are the CEO, a customer service representative or a van driver, you must model your values. Everyone needs to walk their own talk.
3. There must be accountability to enforce the values, based not on positional authority, but on mutual accountability throughout the organization to hold those values in place. We all must be willing to give each other feedback, both positive and negative, to reinforce our values. You must advocate your values, your beliefs, your principles to anyone who will listen.
4. Leaders must systematically teach their values to others. You cannot expect your employees to pick up your values by osmosis. You need to regularly and systematically explain what you believe and why you believe it.

....

You must *make decisions that are consistent with your stated values and mission.*

Here are four ideas for how to make value-honored decisions:

1. Collectively *identify* core values. Sit down as a team and agree upon those things that matter most. Is it trust? Is it respect? Is it fairness? Is it personal responsibility? Is it open and honest communication?

2. *Define* your core values. What does each value or principle mean? Don't assume that everyone understands your values the same way. For example, some people think that respect must be earned; others think they should have respect as soon as they walk in the door; still others would say that respect naturally goes along with a position of authority. If one person thinks respect must be earned, while another thinks respect naturally goes with a person or a position, you're going to have some collisions. Define your core values so that everyone is focused in the same way.

    When you sit down to define your values, don't have a dictionary in the room. You must

....

cause people to think. *Define* trust; define personal responsibility; define fairness; define whatever your core values are. It doesn't matter what the dictionary says. What matters is each definition of a value that your team can understand and agree on.

As you begin to define each of your values, you will get some interesting glimpses into your employees' ideas and values. For example, in one group I worked with, one of the people wanted to define *honesty* as "timely full disclosure." Not simply full disclosure, but *timely* full disclosure. Others in the room were willing to settle for "full disclosure" but maybe fudge a little bit on the time factor. You can see the problems that could arise if everyone is not defining their values in precisely the same way.

To facilitate the process of defining your values, it can be helpful to identify role models for the values you are defining. Make a list of your values and then write the name of a role model next to each value.

3. Once you have all your team's values identified and defined, check all your current systems (pay systems, hiring practices, your other processes)

....

to see if they support your values. It's one thing to say "we believe in fairness," but what are we really saying if we pay two people in the same job two different wages? Are your systems consistent with your values? Are you walking the talk?

4. Understand what is necessary to make decisions that are consistent with your values. Start by asking yourself the following questions:

- What would your role model do?
- What would you do if your kids were watching you—would it be any different?
- What if everyone else did what you are about to do?
- Would you act differently if a TV news crew was outside your door?
- What would Superman do?
- What are your self-alert systems telling you? Your gut? Your conscience?
- Who will be impacted by your decision? How?

Now that your thinking is headed in the right direction, here are seven principles to further guide your decision making:

....

- Follow the Golden Rule: Do unto others as you would have them do unto you.
- Always challenge necessity. Avoid thinking, "This is the only choice I have," or "This is the only way to do this." If someone brings you two choices, look for a third. Focus your thinking on *all* the options. Discuss the good, bad, and interesting aspects of each option. It may take time that you don't have, but if you work with other people, you have to *take* the time to teach, *take* the time to explain, *take* the time to advocate your values.
- Let the long term trump the short term. It's not how you start, it's how you finish that matters. Be there for the long haul. The greatest talent is perseverance.
- Let your core ethical values trump all others. If it ever comes down to violating a core value, the decision is a no-brainer. Don't do it! Decision making is easy once your values are crystal clear.
- Operational values are subject to constant change when there is no foundation of core values to anchor to. Make sure values are consistent between departments—otherwise conflict is inevitable.

••

These last two principles I learned from Michael Josephson, who always said,

- "Principled decision making and ethics is about making better decisions more often. It has nothing to do with being perfect."
- "If it is clearly necessary to violate one core value in order to honor another—if you find it is necessary to violate *respect* because you believe in *fairness*, for example—make the choice that you sincerely believe will do the greatest good in the long run. Deferring to a higher value is the only reason we will violate one of our core values."

Asking yourself …

*Am I secure in who I am
regardless of my performance?*

feeds the Hungers of the Heart by
developing the habit of …

Inner Peace

Am I Secure in Who I Am Regardless of My Performance?

•••••••••••••••••••••••••••••••••

*What lies before us and what lies behind us
are small matters compared to what lies within
us. And when we bring what is within out into
the world, miracles happen.*

—Henry David Thoreau

I don't know about you, but as Speakerman I always tracked my contribution to this world in numeric terms. I always evaluated my worth and determined my value based on performance. I found that if my performance was up my value was up. And if my performance was a little off my self-worth tended also to suffer. This

....

was a constant roller coaster ride that I had to learn to stop. I began searching for ways to feel secure about my self-worth regardless of my performance.

A few years ago, I had my dream job. Not only did I love what I was doing, but I had the perks, the salary— everything was wonderful. Then one day the boss called me into his office and said, "This just isn't working out for us, I'm afraid we'll have to let you go." Just like that, I was fired from my dream job.

I don't know what you would do, but I squared my shoulders good and proud, I looked him right in the eye, and then I cried. And I cried all the way home. I didn't know how I was going to tell Terri that I had just been fired. We had only been in our new home nine months. I had talked Terri into buying a new car, and our first child, Kenda, was only three months old.

I began thinking less and less of myself as I drove home. I kept thinking to myself what a failure I was and I started crying all over again. But you know what, a funny thing happened when I got home. I found out I was more than my job. I found out even though I was rejected at work, my wife still loved me, I was still a dad and I was still a child of God. I hadn't stopped being a neighbor or a friend either, I had just lost a job, that's all. I discovered there is a permanent sense of self worth that you and I need to hold onto. *Your value and my value are not determined by what we do or don't do. Our value has everything to do with who we are.*

Who are you? _____

_____

I used to answer that question in one word: Speakerman. If you answered that question by writing down what you do for a living, I'd like to expand your vision. You need to see yourself in ways that encompass all of your life roles and feed all the Hungers of the Heart. Focus on the unchanging things about who you are for just a minute. If you're a working parent who has just lost your job, look at what you've got. You're Mom, or Dad, you're a spouse, a friend, and a child of God. Those things that are more permanent and of greater value than your job didn't change. You and I need gentle reminders to strengthen our sense of self-worth.

Now, before you go on, take another crack at that question.

Who are you? _____

_____

....

If nothing else, take your sense of lasting worth from the fact that you are and will always be a child of God—handmade in his image. Have you ever made anything with your hands? The pride and the joy of a completed handmade project is something I used to know little about. It has been said of me that I must have had a mechanical bypass because I'm not that great with tools.

One day, when my kids wanted a gym set in the back yard, we went to Sears to get one. We picked out a nice one they could use for years to come and inquired as to the installation cost. I almost had a heart attack when the salesman told me that the installation was over half again as much as the cost of the gym set.

Not wanting to part with the cash (it's also been said that copper wire was invented when someone tried to take a penny from me), and still wanting to get my kids their gym set, I volunteered to assemble this monster myself. You should have seen the looks on our kids' faces. They knew their daddy wasn't exactly handy with tools. Kenda tugged on my sleeve and said, "Daddy are you sure?"

"Sure I'm sure," I said. Then I asked for an idea of the types of tools I would need. A drill, a socket set, a hacksaw, a screwdriver and a ton of patience—most of

which I didn't have. But I did say that I would do this
and "I will do this," I said.

I found out the meaning of manhood with this
project. I thought you were a man when you got
married, or when you had you first child and bought a
home. No-o-o-o....I found out you're not a real man
until you own tools.

I bought my first set of manhood-enhancing
tools. There were only eighty-four bolts to this gym set
and the instructions were pretty detailed. But, not
being mechanically inclined, I took a little longer than
what is normal. Two weeks later...my kids were
swinging in the back yard and I've got to tell you,
watching them swing on something I put together
made me proud.

There are times, to this day, that I will go out into
the back yard and just stare at my creation with absolute
awe and think, "Ohh, Ohh, Ohh, look at what I built
with my own two hands." I finally know what it means
to make something that brings so much joy and make it
with your own hands.

I also think that's how God feels. When he looks
down from heaven and sees us, his created beings
running around bringing joy to others, I'm sure he just
sits back with pride and says, "Ohh, Ohh, Ohh, I built

....

those with my own two hands." Things mean more when they are built by hand.

In Genesis, the scriptures teach that God "took" the dust of the earth to "make" Adam and he "took" the rib from Adam to "make" Eve. Man and woman handmade by God and full of eternal value—that's us. We are all handmade by God and nothing can ever take that away. Don't you see that your value is not in what you do or don't do, but it's in who you are? You are handmade by God, so am I, and once we realize that we will never doubt our self worth ever again.

Now does all this talk of changeless self worth mean you should stop performing at high levels? Not on your life. You should continue to work hard to lead the field with your achievements but if you do fail, you are not a failure. *Failure is an event, not a person.* What God makes has eternal value. Your value and worth are constant, even though your performance may not be.

Lead yourself to show the signs of knowledge of your own changeless value by...

- smiling a lot
- forgetting about beating others to that great parking space

....

- opening yourself up to the love of others by loving them more
- trusting others more
- engaging in dialogue with those not like yourself in order to find common ground
- taking the actions of others at face value instead of trying to find their hidden motives
- learning to enjoy the moment instead of orchestrating the moment

Life is good if you let go and let God show you how to see your true worth through his eyes.

Asking yourself …

Did I schedule some quiet time today?

feeds the Hungers of the Heart by developing the habit of …

Reflection

Did I Schedule Some Quiet Time Today?

●●●●●●●●●●●●●●●●●●●●●●●●●●●●●●

What great luck for rulers that men do not think.

—Adolf Hitler

Most people don't think. It's not that they can't think. It's just that they are so busy, they don't take time to think. Have you ever gone to work and not consciously thought about what it was you were doing? You just kind of sit down at your desk, the phone rings and boom, you're off fighting fires at the crisis du jour.

You put out one fire here and another flares up over there. After a while you see yourself only as a firefighter because that's what you do all day. And you spend so much time fighting these fires, you often have no energy left for the other roles in your life. You become so irritable after a day like this that you begin to think of home as the place you go when you're tired of being nice to people at work.

It is not necessary to continue to work this way—I'd like to give you a competitive edge. This edge will help you outmaneuver your competitors and be blissfully happy at home. Are you ready? Here it comes. *Stop and build time in your schedule to think.* I can guarantee you a competitive advantage, because your competitors are probably running around reacting to their own firefighting moments instead of challenging themselves to think differently.

Here is a story about J. Winthrop III, a man of my imagination, to illustrate the value of thinking differently. Winthrop was wealthy. He drove up in front of the First National Bank of downtown Manhattan in his Rolls Royce sedan. He was seeking a bank that would give him a two-week, two-hundred-dollar loan. He told a loan officer his wishes and the loan officer said, "Are you serious?"

"Yes, I'm serious and I've got collateral," explained Winthrop, as he produced the clear title to the

....

Rolls and insisted the loan be secured with the car. Wanting to earn Winthrop's business and knowing of the occasional idiosyncrasies of the wealthy, the loan officer agreed. Winthrop took the two-hundred-dollar loan, and asked to leave the car at the bank, since it was collateral. The loan officer agreed.

Two weeks later, Winthrop came back and asked what he owed. The loan officer said, "The two-hundred-dollar principal and eighty-seven cents in interest." Winthrop handed over the same hundred dollar bills from two weeks earlier, pulled eighty-seven cents from his pocket and asked for the title to the vehicle, and the car keys. The loan officer walked Winthrop out to his car and asked, "Mr. Winthrop, why did you come in here for a two-week, two-hundred-dollar loan?

Winthrop replied, "Young man, where else in downtown Manhattan could I park my car, leave it for two weeks and have it only cost me eighty-seven cents?"

Winthrop knew how to think differently. You can do the same. But *how do you think differently?* Start by thinking about the things that are important to you during times of quiet reflection and solitude. You can't think differently with the radio on or with the noise clutter in the office. It's got to be quiet. I like to do my thinking in the morning. I go into my office before anyone else, put on an ocean-sounds CD, review my efforts from yesterday and go over what I want to accomplish today. I also pray.

Prayer is a perfect thinking tool because it gets your mind centered on gratitude, faith in God, and the thing I need the most help with—humility. I define humility as a healthy self-respect for my insignificance. Many times, my quiet time in prayer has helped me regain my humility. And anytime I get too cocky, I always remember a story about Muhammad Ali. It is reported that he was on board an aircraft, on his way to defend his heavyweight boxing title, when a flight attendant reminded him to buckle his seat belt. Ali, being a brash man with a habit of calling himself The Greatest, looked at the flight attendant and said, "I'm Superman, and Superman doesn't need a seat belt." The flight attendant looked back at the champ and said, "Superman doesn't need an airplane, you'd better buckle up." Ali buckled up—and he may have learned an important lesson about humility.

When I pray, I reflect back on the Lord's Prayer and the three C's it teaches:

....

- *Compliment* God for all he's done. Nothing builds more humility than stacking yourself up next to God. This idea of complimenting God also helps you to take stock in your blessings and reinforce a greater sense of gratitude before him.
- *Confess* your sins to God. All of us sin. No one will ever live a life good enough to get to heaven because they have not sinned. And because we have all sinned, we all need forgiveness and a savior.
- Share your *Concerns* with him. It's amazing what happens when you just share with God what your concerns and problems are, and see how willing he is to pour out blessings upon us. Ask him, share with him and learn from him as you allow him to walk with you through your life.

All of this can be done quickly on the way to a meeting—or in quiet solitude, and in great detail. Sometimes I just spend all of my thinking time in prayer for my concerns that day. And other times, I may just pray in a free-form style that is more abstract, about anything that comes to mind. The point is that as children of God, you and I need a sense of spiritual stability in our lives if we are to finish well.

You also need *a place to think.* Where is that place for you? I enjoy going to hotel ballrooms where there is a fountain and a beautiful view to look at. There is also a botanical garden in Dallas where I spend a good bit of time just walking around and thinking. A favorite place to think is important because it begins to build an expectation of good thoughts. Every time I go to this place, I expect to walk away with something of great value being revealed to me and it most always happens that way.

In addition to taking time to think and having a place to think, you need *thought starters.* Thought starters are the rich reading material that leads you to apply what you've read in another way. I enjoy reading *Fast Company* magazine, The Bible, *The Wall Street Journal, Fortune,* and *Golf Digest*—or daily devotionals, such as "In His Grip," "One-Minute Businessman's Devotional" or "My Utmost for His Highest." These thought starters function for me as a bridge, which gets me out of the urgency and confusion of today's concerns and lets me focus on the clarity and peace of tomorrow's promises from God.

My good friend Bill Cantrell, author of *Finding Your Direction,* taught me how to start every day by

....

asking three questions of God and waiting to see where those questions took my thinking. Bill taught me to focus on God's kingdom first by asking, "Who would you have me contact in support of and in service to you today?"

Next, I would seek direction and blessing by asking, "Who would you have me contact to build my business and to fulfill the dream you've given me?"

Finally, Bill taught me to focus on practicality by asking God, "What activities would you have me put my hands to today that would make my dream real?" These thought starters have been critical in providing me with the wisdom and insight necessary to lead others and they can do the same for you. Start your day with Bill's thought starters and see for yourself the difference they make.

You also need *thought sculptors*—people in your life who stretch your thinking and help you process issues you're struggling with. Thought sculptors can be a mentor or a friendly competitor. They can be a good friend that you've had for years or someone you've just met. The most important attribute of a thought sculptor is that they have a unique perspective that you trust. You can go to them in confidentiality and be frank about our issues of the heart and know that they won't just help you make a decision, they will also bring a perspective that might otherwise tend to be overlooked.

What are your thought starters? Who are your thought sculptors? Where is your place to think and pray? How often do you stop and think? All of us could stay ahead of the game if we just took more time to think. Take some time to think differently today in your own special quiet time.

Asking yourself ...

What did I do to show my family that I love them?

feeds the Hungers of the Heart by developing the habit of ...

Visible Love

What Did I Do to Show My Family That I Love Them?

•••••••••••••••••••••••••••••••

Providing for your family and intensely loving them is good but it's not enough. You must be there.

—Dr. Beck Weathers

It's important for you to show your family your love, not just tell them about it. Telling them is also important, but if you don't do anything to show them that you love them, your words will lose their effect on their hearts. You must learn to practice the habit of visible love. Visible love is the Habit of the Heart that says providing financially for your family is good...loving your family is good...saying I love you is good...but it's still not enough.

Dr. Gary Chapman has written a book called *The Five Love Languages,* in which he says there are five ways that we express love to each other and one of these five ways is your primary love language. What a great book! The five languages of love are:

1. Acts of Service
2. Words of Encouragement
3. Gift Giving
4. Spending Time Together
5. Personal Closeness or Touching

That last one is my language of love. I'm a hugger. In my family we hug when one of us leaves the room. If Collin says, "Daddy, I'm going to get my pajamas on," I'll respond by saying, "Okay son, come here and give me a big hug before you go down the hall."

When he comes back a few minutes later and says, "Daddy, I've got my pajamas on," I'm apt to say, "Okay son, come over here and give Daddy a big hug." I'm into that—hugs and closeness and touching are how I express my love, in my primary love language.

•••

My wife's primary love language is acts of service, so right away you can see we're on a collision course with each other if she does things for me but I never do anything for her except hug. In my mind, I'll approach Terri thinking, "I want to be near you, c'mon give me a big hug." Meanwhile, in the back of her mind she's thinking of all the things she did for me that day and unspoken questions begin to flood her mind. When was the last time he did the dishes after I cooked? Why didn't he help me yesterday when I had that horrible day at work? Did he help me get the kids to bed?

I don't want to *do* anything, I just want to be with her. But she's thinking, "I don't need you hanging over my shoulder, I want you to help me." We were prime candidates for a train wreck until we learned to understand this. My job is to mold myself into her primary language, her job is to mold herself into my primary love language and together we can give to each other in a way that the other wants. What have you done to show your family how much you love them? If you don't know what their primary love language is, that's okay. Start by taking time to be together.

We have a little custom in my home. When the weather is nice, my kids like to go to the park near our house. When we go to the park, while the kids are

....

playing on the monkey bars, I'll go over to the swings and drop a little pocket change—quarters, nickels and dimes—on the ground. When the kids go to the swings, I run back over to the monkey bars and drop a little more pocket change. They never see me, but when they come off those swings and they land…

"Daddy! Look! A quarter! I found a quarter!" Collin squeals.

Then I'll say to Kenda, "Why don't you go over to the monkey bars." A minute or so later I'll hear, "Daddy! Looky, looky! I found a quarter too!"

This has happened so often in my family that my kids call this place "the money park." They don't know it's me leaving that money, but later on when they find out it was me, they'll know their daddy loved them because he showed them he loved them, and he showed them a lot. He gave them reasons to believe his words when he said, "I love you." I'm not suggesting that money is the only way to show your kids that you love them. The point is, it's usually the little things that show your family that you love them and show them how special they are to you.

Here are twenty-one ways you can show your family how much you love them. For frequent-flying fathers or mommies on the move, first a warning.… A lifestyle centered around your work is devastating for family stability. Short-term periods of intensity are understandable and often unavoidable. The following tips are meant as a stop-gap measure during these seasons of intensity and under no circumstances am I providing these as an alternative to you being physically and emotionally present at home. That being understood, here are some ways you can include your family in your travels:

1. Put the family activities that your spouse and kids want to do on your office calendar and once it's scheduled, make it inviolate by you or anyone in the office.

2. Make sure that at least once a week you have at least two hours of one-on-one time with each child and with your spouse before you engage in any activities for yourself.

3. Buy a disposable camera and take it along as a way of sharing your business travel experiences with your family.

4. E-mail your spouse and kids while online with your business correspondence.

5. Carry the most recent pictures of your family and place them on the nightstand or dresser in your hotel room.

....

6. Have the kids fax you their drawings and homework from school.

7. Use a push-pin map of the United States or the world so your kids can see where you are going and all of the places you have been.

8. Order room service for breakfast, then call your family and share breakfast over the phone.

9. Put an extra one hundred dollars in your spouse's purse or wallet with a sticky-note that says, "Surprise!"

10. Encourage your family to leave you voice-mail messages. Save them, so when you're working late you can call and still hear their voices even after they've gone to sleep.

11. Once a year, take your family on one of your nicer business trips.

12. When you get back into town after your trip, rather than going straight to the office, pop in on your kids at school and see if you can take your spouse to lunch for just a few moments alone.

13. Cook a big breakfast for everyone and clean up after.

14. Read to your kids even after they say they're too old for it.

15. Help your children with their homework no matter how tired you are.

16. Never give your kids cause to think that work or the TV is more important than they are.

17. Help your children plant a candy garden. Cultivate a little two-foot-square space of soil and plant rows of sugar cubes. Let the kids water them once a day for a week and on the last night, stick their favorite candy in the rows and watch the joy of that harvest the next morning.

18. During the school year, let your kids sleep in. Call the office and tell them you won't be in. When your kids come down the hall panicking because they've realized they're supposed to be at school, tell them, "Today is a snow day!" When they go to the window and see no snow, tell them you declared today a snow day and there will be no work for you and no school for them but whatever they want to do is what the day is for. What a memory maker this idea is!

19. Call your spouse's best friends and arrange for everyone to meet you and your spouse for lunch or dinner.

....

20.   Probably the best thing any of us can do for any
       of our family members is slow down, listen to
       them and try to see things through their eyes.
21.   When asked, "So...what do you do?" introduce
       yourself as a spouse or a parent before telling
       others what you do professionally.

      Layer upon layer, day after day, these little expres-
sions of love begin to make a difference. Remember,
what counts is that you take the time to do the little
things. What have you done to show your family that
you love them? Focus on that each and every day.

Asking yourself ...

Did I keep my commitments at home?

feeds the Hungers of the Heart by developing the habit of ...

Faithfulness

Did I Keep My Commitments at Home?

• •

*Nobody ever went to their death bed saying
I wish I had more time at the office.*

—Peter Lynch

I bet I know what kind of parent you are. You're
the kind of parent who wants his kids to...

- Obey the law and stay in school
- Say no to drugs, alcohol abuse and risky
  behavior
- Stand firm against unhealthy peer pressure
- Get good grades in school and go on to college

• Earn the respect of teachers and peers
• Know Mommy and Daddy love them

Those kinds of kids don't grow up that way without you being there to teach them how. But you say, "Wait a minute, you don't know how important my job is." Your kids don't know how important your job is either. You're not the regional VP to them. They don't care that the product launch is in three months or that the IPO is coming up. To them, you are Mom or Dad. *All they know is if you are not going to be there for them, everything else is irrelevant.* As parents, we've got to get that message.

I had the great pleasure to get to meet Dr. Norman Vincent Peale. Even into his nineties, Dr. Peale had a quick wit and a Wealthy Heart that inspired everyone he met. One of Dr. Peale's legendary stories is about a parent who reluctantly kept his commitments at home, and learned the value of that decision.

The story begins with a forty-three-year-old businessman rushing down the stairs at six o'clock on a Saturday morning. He was filled with enthusiasm because he was going out for a long-awaited round of golf with his best friend and business partner. They hadn't played in about five months. As he was getting his clubs ready and getting his breakfast fixed, his twelve-year-old son rushed downstairs equally filled with enthusiasm. The dad looked at the boy and said, "What are you so excited about?" The young man grinned at his dad and said, "Oh Dad, this is going to be a great day. I can't wait to go fishing with you this morning."

The father suddenly remembered the commitment he had made to his son about a month earlier. The boy looked at his father's expression and said, "What's the matter Dad?"

His father replied, "Oh nothing, son, I just need to make a phone call." True to his word, the man made the phone call and canceled the important golf game. But he was more than a little resentful at missing such an opportunity. His business partner had been a mentor to him, and they were able to process all kinds of thoughts while playing golf. He really wanted to be there with his friend, but he had made a promise to his twelve-year-old son.

He went and changed clothes, and they hooked up the boat and went out to the lake. They cast their lines to the left and they cast their lines to the right, but not many fish were biting that day. One hour stretched to four hours of patient sitting. They exchanged little bits of cordial conversation, but nothing like what he would have accomplished had he been on the golf course with his partner.

Finally, with nothing to show for their day of fishing, not even a really good bite, father and son hooked up the boat and drove back home pretty much in silence. Dad went upstairs to his room and the boy went over to his.

The dad was grumbling to himself about having wasted the day, when his wife came into the room, with a tear in her eye. He glanced at her and said, "What's wrong?"

"Oh nothing," she replied, "I was just reading our son's entry in his journal for today. He gave it to me to read."

The man kind of snorted and said, "Yeah, you should see my entry: 'Four hours sittin' in a boat, doin' nothing. Big whoop.'"

Without a word, his wife handed him the young man's journal and asked him to read it. The dad looked down and read the following words: "Spent the best day of my life today, with Dad."

When the man read those words, his eyes suddenly got a little watery, but his vision became crystal clear. You see, those words didn't change his mind—they changed his heart.

How about you? When was the last time you said no to something important in the office so you could keep a family commitment? Remember, twenty years from now you won't remember the pressing matters that kept you away from your family events, but your kids will never forget the fact that you weren't there. Be there for them. Your family commitments really are more important than any business commitment you'll ever keep. When you make a commitment to your family, keep it. Steven Covey, author of *The Seven Habits of Highly Effective People,* said that anybody who ever came into his office fully understood that if a family member walked in the door, the meeting was over.

Covey has the right idea. You may be saying, "I'm not a best-selling author and I can't afford to make that kind of decision." Covey made those decisions before anybody knew who he was. The reason people pay attention to him today is because he made the commitment twenty years ago. What will you decide to do?

The June 1998 edition of *Dallas Child Magazine* tells the story of Ron Kirk, a committed father and husband who served as Mayor of Dallas, Texas. The city was having its largest-ever bond election to build a more attractive downtown area for citizens and convention-

....

eers. "That vote was probably the biggest political test of my life," Kirk said, but the mayor had a previous engagement on his calendar. Everyone who knew Ron Kirk knew he always reserved the weekends for his family but this was an election weekend. Would things be any different?

His daughter's very last Indian Princess Campout was being held that weekend, but Kirk never wavered on his decision. On the biggest election day of his career, Kirk went to camp. "There will be other elections but there won't be another last Indian Princess Campout," he observed.

All children want to look out and see their parents at special school events. It doesn't matter if you are the president of the United States, if you've got kids at the school play, those kids of yours expect you to be fighting for position with the camcorder like every other parent.

You don't have to be president, or mayor, or a best-selling author to say no at work and yes to your family. All you have to be is committed to your customers at home and place them in higher esteem than your customers at work.

Terri and I established our married life on five words that help us keep our commitments to each other.

Before we got married, Terri looked at me and I looked at her and I said, "Baby, you know, about this marriage thing—there are 1.2 million divorces every year. My family has a lot of chaos and divorce in it and so has yours. It's like the deck is stacked against us but I really want this to be a forever kind of commitment."

"I know," she said, "so what if we lived our married life based on five words?"

"What do you mean five words?" I asked. "What are the five words?"

She looked at me and smiled, and said, "There is no way out."

I believe commitment comes down to these five words: *There is no way out.* That's a pretty powerful set of words. You see, when there is no way out, you stop wasting your energy looking for a way out instead of focusing on making things better where you are. When there is no way out, you learn to work together.

Of course, it only works as long as both people remain committed to the idea that there is no way out. Periodically, Terri and I will pass each other in the hallway and she'll give me the look. You know what look I'm talking about. The one that stops you dead in your tracks and makes you say, "What?"

••

Terri will just smile and say, "Just checking. There's still no way out, right?"

"Yep, still no way out."

Family is more important than work. Keep your commitments at home.

Asking yourself …

Did I protect my honesty and integrity?

feeds the Hungers of the Heart by developing the habit of …

Trustworthiness

Did I Protect My Honesty and Integrity?

• •

Your honesty and integrity is your greatest business asset. You've got to focus on protecting your honesty and integrity, especially as leaders.

Ask yourself this soul-searching question: What is the foundation of leadership? What is that powerful influence called leadership built on?

David Kerns, former CEO of Xerox and former Undersecretary of State, had this to say: "It is absolutely imperative that we have people coming up into the leadership corps of our country, who really understand the issue of integrity."

••

As I travel around today, I'm finding there are fewer and fewer people who really, deeply, honestly, sincerely understand the issue of integrity.

Bob Crandall, former chairman of AMR (American Airlines) says, "You've got to have the highest ethical standards to be an effective leader."

You have to be a role model and you must create an atmosphere of ethical behavior throughout your organization. So your foundation of leadership is integrity, ethical behavior, and "walking the talk."

Dick Gelb, the legendary CEO of Bristol-Meyers Squibb, simply says it this way: "The years the big companies have gotten into trouble, their people were receiving two messages at the same time." The first message was the high-road approach—"We won't stand for this type of unethical behavior." The other message was, "You're really behind on your budget right now, and we're expecting you to make it. Don't tell me how you do it, just do it!" With those mixed messages, people are apt to do strange things.

Everybody talks about integrity. I always ask people, "What does integrity mean?" Often they don't have a firm answer. They know they want integrity in the workplace but they can't quite define it. How will you know it when you see it if you can't define it?

....

Take a minute to write your own definition of integrity. Don't cheat and use the dictionary. Instead, think about your own values and define integrity:

_____

_____

_____

_____

Integrity must be based on your values. Integrity is about wholeness, it's about completeness, it's about always holding yourself accountable to whatever your values are. You must first understand what your values are, so that you can have integrity to those values. And your values should be ethical values—values that are good, helpful and universally embraced. If you don't tie your integrity to ethical values, what you end up accomplishing may not be good. We can say that Hitler had integrity, because he followed through on what he believed. We can say that David Koresh had integrity, because he had one-hundred-percent, total focus on his value system.

I disagree with both of their value systems, but the point is if you talk about integrity, you have to talk about the value system that your integrity is attached to.

• •

Everybody wants people who are honest and trustworthy. Companies want people they know they can count on, and people with a good sense of commitment. Do you know what commitment means? You're not going to get commitment until their hearts are engaged. You may get compliance—but you can inspire commitment if you have a Wealthy Heart. People have to believe that you honestly mean what you say.

Asking yourself …

Did I read or learn anything new?

feeds the Hungers of the Heart by
developing the habit of …

Learning

Did I Read or Learn Anything New?

●●●●●●●●●●●●●●●●●●●●●●●●●●●●●●

The Internet and the Web are wonderful resources you can use to learn new things. I look at the interactive edition of *The Wall Street Journal* every day. I also read the *New York Times, Business Week,* and *Fortune,* all digitally presented now. What a wonderful world it is. There's a great web site I've fallen in love with called Answers.com. You can ask them anything, and for a fee in the range of three to ten dollars, they'll find the answer for you. What an empowering world it is that we live in. What have you done today to read or learn things that are new to you?

Sometimes you learn something new just by getting into a taxicab. I met a cab driver once who

....

proved to me the power of thinking creatively. If you've attended one of my seminars you've heard me talk about Les Jones.

What do most cab drivers do? They troll around the airports, they troll around the hotels, and they kind of wait on a reactive basis for somebody to say, "Hey, I need a ride." Not Les Jones.

I was flying to a conference on a 2:00 P.M. flight from Dallas–Fort Worth. I called Executive Cab Company in Dallas to get a ride. I told the dispatcher that I needed the cab to arrive at 1:00 P.M., because it takes me almost exactly one hour to get from my office to the airport, and I needed the time up until 1:00 P.M. to get ready to go on that trip.

At 12:30 P.M. the receptionist at the front desk called me and said, "Your cab is here." I glanced at my watch and my blood pressure instantly went up. I appreciated the cab driver arriving early, but I really needed that last half-hour to finish getting ready. I said, "Tell the guy I need until one o'clock to get all these details closed up before I leave."

She relayed the message and I went back to work. About two minutes later, the receptionist called me again. "The cab driver is asking if there's anything he can do for you while he waits."

....

I said, "What can a cab driver do for me?"

She said, "I don't know, but he's asking me if there is anything he can do. Do you need any errands done?"

"Are you serious?"

"Yes," she replied.

I had to meet this guy! I went out to the front desk and he handed me his business card. A cab driver with a business card, and not just any business card, either. His was exceptional. This was a picture of the cab driver sitting on the hood of his car, with the skyline of Dallas in the background, and he's holding his two pet poodles. As I looked at the card, I saw his marketing phrase at the bottom, which really set off bells and whistles for me. His name was Les Jones and down there at the bottom it said, "You always get more with Les."

Here was a cab driver taking the time to understand how to market himself more effectively. I was so impressed, I grabbed all my stuff and said, "Let's go, I want to talk to you."

We went out front, I hopped into the cab, and there was a fresh newspaper, the *Dallas Morning News*. I said, "This is really incredible—what a life."

As the cabby slid behind the wheel, he said, "What do you mean?"

....

I said, "There's a fresh paper in the back seat of your cab. Here it is almost 1:00 in the afternoon and I'm probably the first customer you've had all day. What a life, coming to work at 1:00 in the afternoon."

He said, "Oh, no, you're mistaken. I give a fresh paper to *everybody* who rides in my cab. Look behind you."

The cab was a station wagon, and when I peered over the back seat I saw a stack of *USA Today* and a stack that was *Dallas Morning News*.

Les Jones said, "I just kind of picked you for a *Dallas Morning News* guy."

All I could say was, "Well Les, I really appreciate that."

I started to read the paper, we were on the way to the airport, and a few minutes later Les said, "Excuse me for interrupting, but do you need a return pickup?"

"A what?"

"A return pickup. Do you need a ride home when you get back?"

I said, "Well, yes, I need a return pickup." I needed a way to get home when I got back. But do you know when I would have thought of that? At thirty-two thousand feet, on approach to Dallas–Fort Worth, about thirty minutes before landing. It finally would have dawned on me that I needed a way home, and I would have had to figure out whom to call. Now I wouldn't need to call. Les Jones set up a return pickup with me, asking me what time I was getting in, and telling me he would meet me at the gate. I said, "Hey Les, I don't get in until 10:30 on Friday night."

He said, "That's okay, I'll meet you at 10:30 on Friday night."

I said, "Now look, don't over-promise and under-deliver. Just tell me if you're going to be here."

He said, "I'll be here."

At 10:30 on Friday night, not expecting him to be there, I walked off the plane. "Hey, Mr. Conley, over here!" Sure enough, there was Les Jones. He grabbed my bags, carried them to the car for me, and took me home. I was impressed.

On the way home, he asked for my business card. I gave it to him and didn't think anything of it until about three months later when I got a Christmas card from Les Jones. I looked at the Christmas card. It had his phone number on it, so I called him right up and I said, "Les, how did you know where to get in touch with me and send your Christmas card?"

He replied, "Don't you remember? You gave me your business card that day and I scanned it into my database."

....

I said, "You did what?

"I took your business card and scanned it into my database."

Les Jones is a cab driver in the Dallas–Fort Worth area who drives around with a laptop computer and a cellular phone in his cab, and he has a by-appointment-only business. You need connections if you want to ride with him. Les Jones knows what it's all about. Learn something new and then apply it at home or at work.

Asking yourself …

Did I laugh today?

feeds the Hungers of the Heart by
developing the habit of …

Fun

Did I Laugh Today?

•••••••••••••••••••••••••••••••••••••

Eagles may soar, but weasels don't get sucked into jet engines.
—Marcus' Benny's Bagels, Carrollton, TX

I hope your day starts out better than one clerk's day at a fast food restaurant. It was the height of the morning rush, about seven o'clock, when a gunman walked up to the counter, pointed his pistol at the clerk and demanded all the money in the cash drawer. The clerk wanted to comply but he couldn't get the cash drawer open. Finally, he realized that the system was set up for cash drawers to open only after food orders were entered.

....

Not thinking, the clerk looked up at the gunman and told him, "You're going to have to order something before the cash drawer will open." It didn't dawn on the clerk that all he had to do was enter an order himself as if a customer had placed an order. The gunman thought the clerk was trying to stall so he became more forceful and threatening in his demands. This only served to bring on more anxiety in the clerk, who continued to plead with the gunman to place a food order so the drawer would open.

Apparently, the gunman became convinced. The next thing that happened was he took two steps back and started to scan the menu board. Making his selection, the gunman stepped back up to the counter and placed his order.

"Get me a double cheeseburger and hurry up!"

The clerk's training kicked in and instinctively and without thinking he asked the gunman, "Do you want fries with that?"

"No, just the double cheeseburger, come on."

Fumbling to key in the order, the clerk became frustrated when the cash drawer refused to open. Over and over again he kept pressing the button for double cheeseburger and nothing happened. The drawer wouldn't open because the double cheeseburger was a

....

lunch menu item and that order couldn't be filled until after 10:30 A.M. The clerk started to cry. The gunman, realizing he couldn't get to the cash without the clerk's compliance, tried to calm the clerk down. The clerk, through his tears, looked up and told the gunman, "You're going to have to order something off the breakfast menu."

The gunman's mouth popped open and stayed open. He couldn't believe how such a simple task had become so difficult to perform. He looked at the clerk with pity and disbelief, exhaled rather forcefully, finally lowered his pistol, and turned and walked out of the store shaking his head as he tried to figure out what went wrong.

How did your day start? Did you wake up this morning like my friend Ernie Lansford and think to yourself, "Today I'll have the time of my life!"

Or do you tend to wake up thinking to yourself, "Oh God! I don't want to go to work today...but I guess I gotta go. Oh, Oh! OH!! How many more sick days have I got left, baby? None?! I GOTTA GO IN?! Oh I hate that job, I hate that job!"

Have you ever met anyone who seems to think this way? Can't you just see him stumbling out of bed in the morning, shuffling down the hallway, pouring down

....

five cups of motivation, then going into work to meet with unsuspecting customers and peers? Author C. W. Metcalf in his book *Lighten Up!* has a phrase he uses to describe those with the sour looks on their faces. He calls them "terminally professional" or TPs for short. TPs view the workplace as a dog-eat-dog world. Their motto is "Bite first and bite hard."

TPs can also be the workaholics of the world who believe that everything revolves around their work. TPs may be successful in business, but most often they fail at friendship, family, faith and fun. Speakerman was a TP. There is no fun at work for TPs because work is a place of business and business is supposed to be competitive, cutthroat and mean. I know too many people like that. Don't be one of them.

Learn to laugh, learn to lighten up and have a good time, especially at work. One of the secrets to living well and sustaining a Wealthy Heart is feeding the hunger to be attracting to others. Now I said *attracting,* not attractive. There's a difference. Not everyone can be attractive physically, but everyone can be attracting, meaning they can develop a spirit about them and a presence that makes others want to be around them.

Preparing yourself to be attracting starts when your eyes open in the morning. The first thing an attracting person with a Wealthy Heart does in the morning is lie in bed and smile. Just smile. Lie there for four or five minutes and get a grin on your face that looks like you just won the lottery. The physical act of smiling seems to encourage an attracting frame of mind.

This next part is going to sound ridiculous, but trust me it works. After you've smiled for a few minutes, let your mind drift until a song comes into your being, a song that lifts your spirit. If you are fortunate enough, you will become so joyous with this tune in your head that you begin to hum or sing out loud. I've got to tell you, one of the most hilarious sights you will ever see is yourself in the mirror early in the morning singing a tune.

Keep in mind that I do not live alone, but if I starting singing every morning chances would be higher that I would be living alone soon. No problem. When I wake up—I don't want to disturb my wife—I just lie there and smile. When the song comes into my head, I mouth the words without singing out loud.

Now, I don't know what song pops into your head when you do this, but for me, my song is…"I got sunshine, on a cloudy day. When it's cold outside, I got the month of May." Motown makes every day better.

....

I also love to sing in elevators. As I'm sure you are aware, people in elevators haven't learned to appreciate the value of elevator singing. Most elevator riders are one of two kinds of people. They are either number watchers or floor watchers. People usually get on elevators, go to the back, turn facing the door and watch either the floor or the numbers. Knowing this, I like to start things off differently.

When I get on an elevator, I get on without turning to face the door, punch my floor and stand in the doorway just far enough in so that the door closes behind me. Now the floor watchers and the number watchers have a dilemma. They don't want any eye contact but their curiosity is creating an internal battle with them. The number watchers struggle to keep from looking me in the eye but since I'm facing toward them, the temptation is too great. Likewise, the floor watchers don't want to look up either but they are almost magnetically pulled to make eye contact with me.

When I lock eyes with the people in the elevator, that's my cue to sing.

"I got sunshine, on a cloudy day. When it's cold outside, I got the month of May." You don't have to sing *My Girl*. You can sing anything, it doesn't matter what you sing, just the fact that you're

....

singing in an elevator is going to seem a little unusual to most people.

I was speaking at a company's annual franchisee meeting in Palm Springs. I got in the elevator by myself and was singing because I was about to speak to fifteen hundred people and I was feeling good. On the way down to the ballroom floor I started snapping my finger, still singing, "I got sunshine..." In the elevator shaft next to me, the elevator was going up and I could hear a deep, manly voice singing back to me, "On a cloudy day!" I didn't know you could hear other people through the elevator shaft. My day was a little brighter after sharing that sunshine in song with that unknown elevator rider.

More of us TPs need to learn to laugh. Laughter engages the heart. The hidden truth is that when the heart is engaged, the mind will follow. But you can't engage someone just intellectually and be guaranteed of his commitment. Some folks have forgotten how to laugh or stopped valuing the healing power of humor because they don't understand it. Humor doesn't fit on a spreadsheet and analysts on Wall Street have no line item for it. Humor is a priceless asset at work because it's a creativity stimulus and is the tool for building relationships that last.

....

Far too many people take their bodies to work but don't bring their commitment, passion and spirit in the door with them. Let laughter happen at work. Find a way to have fun no matter what you do for a living.

Two Role Models of Fun at Work

Let's see how high the bar has been raised against having fun at work. Recently, two of our major home appliances needed repair. We called Sears. The person I got on the phone obviously knew how to have fun at work. Our conversation started:

"Sears Repair Center."

"We need help with our Kenmore appliances, can you get someone out here today?"

"Yes sir, we probably can. What's your phone number?"

I told him my phone number.

"Is this Jeff Conley?"

"Yes."

"Do you still live at…?"

"Yes."

"Are these the appliances you bought in 1988?"

"Yes and I must say I'm amazed that you know so much about me."

"Oh, that's not all. My computer tells me your daughter's about to get a D in English."

This guy was just having fun. And think of his work environment. If he's lucky he's got a color monitor to stare at all day. I can see the strong possibility that he's working in a tight cubicle having to filter out the conversations of his coworkers just a few feet away. Yet, even in that kind of an environment, this champion still wants to connect with customers and have fun. He's a winner with a winner's attitude that would be a welcome addition to any team.

Now look at Southwest Airlines. They have an unparalleled record of performance in a relentless and savagely competitive industry. Yet, they have found a way to have fun because they realize that while technology can be duplicated, the spirit of people can not. At Southwest it's okay to have fun.

I called Southwest recently, to order some tickets over the phone and found out first hand just how different they are. When you call in to order tickets, no matter what air carrier you call you're always put on hold. Many companies see putting you on hold as an opportunity to market to a captive prospect. As you are

....

holding, recorded messages about the latest and greatest offers pour out over the phone. Not at Southwest. They are different.

Once while I was holding for a Southwest agent, I had been waiting for about two minutes when a recorded voice came on the line and said, "Hey." Needless to say, this was something I didn't expect but I knew it was a recording and didn't answer. The voice came back on and this time it said the same thing a little more forcefully. I listened intently and the voice said, "You've probably been on hold a while so if you want to you can press three. Now it's not going to do anything, but it'll probably make you feel better if you press three."

While taking the flight with Southwest, I saw that the fun doesn't just happen over the phone. The flight attendants were laughing and having fun during their safety demonstration. "Okay Ladies and Germs, what I'm about to say is important and failure to listen to me could result in your premature death." Everyone on the plane suddenly began paying attention to the safety demo. At the end of the demo, the flight attendant said, "We'll be on our way shortly and we hope you have a great flight. But if you don't have a good flying experience with us just tell everyone you flew Delta."

....

I laughed and enjoyed the big-picture message. Even if you lead your industry, don't take yourself so seriously that you can't be attracting to customers. Use humor to break down barriers and build bridges of hope between people. I'm not telling you that Southwest succeeds because they know how to have fun at work. But I can guarantee you they are making more money having fun than they ever would as a team of TPs. Find a way to laugh at work every day.

Asking yourself …

Was I a model of excellence at work today?

feeds the Hungers of the Heart by developing the habit of …

Staying in Demand

Was I a Model of Excellence at Work Today?

• •

Man who wait for roast duck to fly in mouth will wait for very long time.
— Ancient Chinese Proverb

My role model, the famed American motivational teacher Zig Ziglar, starts every one of his seminars with the same question, "How many of you believe there is something you could do in the next seven days that would make your personal or professional life worse?" Big laughs, and hands go up all around the arena. Zig goes on to say, "Then I'm sure you will agree that there is also something you can do in the next seven days that will make things better. Which will you choose, better or worse?"

We all want to be better both at work and at home. Let's focus on work for a moment. How can you be a model of excellence at work? I think it starts by seeing yourself as an example of excellence. All employers want the same thing in their people. After working with over five hundred different companies and talking with hundreds of executives, I can tell you, they all pretty much want the same things. What they want are people who are:

- More flexible in meeting customer demands
- Able to evolve, work hard and stay on the cutting edge
- More creative
- Service centered
- Proactive problem solvers
- Open, honest and fear-free communicators
- Emotionally mature people they can trust
- Able to create a unity of spirit
- Not afraid to learn from failure
- Supportive, and respectful of the value of people
- Possessors of a sense of urgency
- Able to stay productive by having fun and building balance

....

Let me hold up a mirror for a minute and ask you a couple of questions. How well do you model these attributes? Would others think of you as an example of excellence in each of these areas?

By the way, employees want these same things from their leadership teams. If you are in a position of authority, how well do you stack up at modeling these qualities? Do your people see you as a boss or a leader? The two are at opposite ends of the same spectrum. What's the difference?

- A boss pushes people from behind—a leader pulls people through from out in front
- A boss gets things done through compliance, getting people to do what they're told to do—a leader is interested in getting commitment
- A boss sees people as tools to help her achieve the objectives she has laid out for herself—a leader sees people as active partners in the process, knowing that only together will they be able to do some things they have never done before
- A boss depends on command and control—a leader depends on trust

....

- A boss talks about values—a leader models them
- A boss is guarded, distant and is never wrong—a leader is vulnerable, genuine and expects open feedback for the good of the organization

There is a huge difference between those two mind-sets. Are you a boss or are you a leader? You need a solid understanding of what leadership is and isn't. Take a minute to write your own definition of leadership. Don't bother using the dictionary, because I can tell you that Webster's says a leader is "one who leads." You're looking for a little better definition than that.

What is leadership? _____

_____

_____

Before I give you my Jeffinition of what leadership is, let's define what it isn't. Leadership is not about exerting power by forcing your will on others with the my-way-or-the-highway approach. Rather than pushing their point of view or forcing their will, leaders seek to build enough trust with their people so that they willingly embrace the values and beliefs of the leader.

I define leadership as a process of influence, plain and simple. Leadership is a process of influence gained by working with people long enough so that they are able to understand three things:

- how much you care about their welfare;
- your vision for the future and the values that will guide the journey; and
- your commitment to being a role model for what you talk about.

Couple this aspect of caring about them with the notion that you have a clearly defined vision for the future and ethical values that are inviolate, and you've got yourself a leader who can take a team anywhere.

Obviously, this type of leadership doesn't automatically come because of a position one has in the company. This type of leadership can be developed by anyone, no matter what job they may have. I've seen people who didn't have the title of Regional VP or Director, but who had power as leaders because of their commitment to people. The key is to gain the respect and trust of a group of people, to the point that the group

....

willingly embraces your values and beliefs—that's leadership. And when the group consistently acts in accordance with those values and beliefs—that's leadership in action.

Remember, you don't have to be the head honcho to be a leader. Influencing, based on trust and respect, can be accomplished by *anyone,* in any organization. And that is true whether the company is a Fortune 500 company, a small independent business, a family or a community. Just go back and review the qualities listed in this chapter and ask yourself every day, "How well did I model those qualities?"

Asking yourself …

Can I rest without being restless?

feeds the Hungers of the Heart by
developing the habit of …

Renewal

Can I Rest without Being Restless?

All work and no play makes Jack a dull boy.
—Jack Nicholson in *The Shining*

Have you ever felt so overwhelmed by demands and deadlines that you felt like a fish swimming in a blender knowing someone was about to press the frappe button? Today many people feel caged by their jobs as they live and work under the constant and invasive influence of technology. No longer the power tool for the elite, technology can be used by almost anybody, anywhere. Incoming calls can reach you in-flight. Nationwide pagers and digital phones collect messages that haunt you until you notice them and

••

retrieve and delete them. One third of America is now wired for technology at home and Microsoft is counting on that statistic to grow. It's not making us better, it's making us busier.

You put in more overtime because it's convenient. For working parents this can create a devastating downward spiral as they get so immersed in the habits of busy-ness at work that they find themselves keeping the same tightly scheduled pace at home. Living the mantra of more is better, we've conditioned ourselves to run from one activity to another, as though Quality Time is a prize to be stalked. While the term burnout used to be reserved for the overworked, today we are seeing burned out parents and spouses who desperately need fresh ideas to help them slow down and renew themselves.

If you have become consumed by the Beast of Busy-ness, there's hope. Here are seven steps to daily renewal and learning to rest without being restless.

- At work, stop thinking of yourself as the cavalry who has to rescue everyone. When you are forever flying to the rescue to save the day, you are cheating others out of their greatest learning opportunities—failure and personal experience.

....

- While giving one hundred and ten percent is appreciated, it also makes common sense that giving one hundred and ten percent for ten days in a row leaves you with nothing left in reserve to give. If you've gone ten days or so without a break don't wait for your body to tell you you're about to collapse. Take some time off NOW!
- There is a natural rhythm to life that we tend to disrupt with our go, go, go, work-centered mentalities. Let's simplify things. All of balanced living and renewal can fit into one of four quadrants—Work, Play, Love and Worship. If you are constantly trying to find a way to have more fun (play) at work or seek to discover spirituality (worship) in the workplace and if you have few or no friends (love) away from work then the Beast of Busyness has got you.

If you are also easily fatigued yet can't seem to get to sleep, the busy-ness has got you. If you feel out of control, can't maintain your focus and have no appetite for either food or sex, Mr. Beast has your number. But hang on. To beat the beast, here's your prescription:

....

- Take time away from work and your other responsibilities to play. Put it in your schedule and protect it. For some reason, we will work all day, then move heaven and earth for our kids to have fun, but deny ourselves day after day. No more! Go play. More effort does not always equal better results. I can guarantee you that better results will come if you learn to regularly free your mind in play.

- Get involved in a local church that is real, alive and loving. The importance of worship can be denied but it can not be ignored. We are all children of God and children need their parents for guidance, direction, sustenance and love. You may think of yourself as being independent of your spiritual father, but there is a deep dependence upon God within us all. Denying that dependence starves your spirit. If you really say you don't need God, then try going without your money. After all, "In God We Trust" is on every bill.

- Don't go it alone. Isolation fosters stress accumulation, disease and premature death. Intimacy with others (love) promotes health. It's hard to meet new friends, but friendship starts with your

••

level of expectancy. I actually approach everyone as being valuable and worthy of respect, because long ago I learned that almost everyone responds to my belief that people I don't know are just friends I haven't met yet. People respond to other people who have that positive expectancy.

- Dial down your stress meter by asking yourself, "Is this really going to matter a month from now?" It's amazing how much emotional clutter we keep. Just let it go if it won't matter next month.

Remember, learning to rest is about balancing Hard Work, Hallelujah, Heart Time, and Hakuna Matata.

Asking yourself …

Did I provide emotional support for my family?

feeds the Hungers of the Heart by developing the habit of …

Being There

Did I Provide Emotional Support for My Family?

•••••••••••••••••••••••••••••••

It's never too late to be what we might have been.

—George Eliot

Provide emotional support for your loved ones by encouraging them, listening to them and telling them that you love them. Be there for them. Turn off the television, even if your team is in the championship game, and put down the paper when your youngsters ask you a question. Set aside work sometimes and play with them when they want you to. There will always be deadlines and more work—but your children, who want your attention now, are going to grow up.

Some years ago, a prominent actor who was highly successful in films won an Academy Award. At the press conference afterwards he was quite overwhelmed and made the comment that his family was important to him but his career was taking off now and these years belonged to him. At the time, he had three kids under twelve years of age and he and his wife had a seventeen-year marriage. *Wrong response!*

You can still find paths of success that allow your family to make the trip with you. Your children are with you for such a little while and you have such a small window of time with them. Learn to make the most of it while you can. This doesn't only apply to celebrities. I've watched many corporate executives follow the career-first path and act as if that path were the only way to go. Night after night, family time gives way to work as these misguided professionals hope that one day their efforts will earn them the praise of superiors and the key to an executive toilet. *Wrong idea!*

So many of us work as if there is a corporate hall of fame in which one day our bust will be on display and people will file by and say, "Oh, there's Conley. He was such a great one. There won't be another one like him. That's why we buried him here at the office." Wake up. The company won't bury you. The company

....

may kill you, but it won't bury you. It's your family that will lay you to rest and when they do, how will you be remembered?

I walked through a cemetery recently and looked for the headstones that said, "Youngest CEO in the history of the company." I looked for the ones that said, "Salesman of the Year, Three Years in a Row!" and "Made the Most Money during His Kids' Years at Home." Of course, I couldn't find any that read that way. What I saw were headstones that read, "Beloved Wife"…"Loving Father"…and "Precious Daughter."

It's our families that miss us when we're gone. Why should they have to miss you while you're still alive? Ask yourself, "What kind of legacy am I leaving my family?" If all you're doing is going to work to make more money, the legacy you'll leave will be in somebody else's checkbook. Think about that. Is that what you want to be remembered for?

The Big Truck Theory

After one of my speeches, a young lady came up to me and asked, "Have you ever heard of the big truck theory?"

• •

I said, "The big truck theory? No, I've never heard of it."

She said, "It's simple. My father taught it to me as a little girl and I've never forgotten it." She went on to explain, "If you get hit and killed by a big truck today, somebody else will be doing your job tomorrow."

"I don't like that thought," I said.

"Well, that's not all," she continued. "Let me tell you the rest of the big truck theory. If you get hit and killed by a big truck today, you will *never* be replaced at home.…You will be missed there *forever.*"

Let that sink in for a minute. When you get home, hug your kids. Kiss your spouse the way you did when you were dating. Tune into their world. If you only focus on satisfying your customers at work, your customers at home may start looking for another supplier. Don't let that happen to you.

Start by being mentally focused on your family and listening to them. Don't just hear them—hearing is a physical function. Listen to them. Listening is a mental function and it says, "I value you enough to work to understand your heart and how you feel."

Encourage your family. Let them know that you value them and take the time to notice what's happening in their lives. Compliment them when things go well and encourage them to learn from their mistakes when things go poorly. Don't be a parent who has all the answers but do be a parent who is emotionally and mentally present when you are at home.

Finally, tell your children how much you love them. Every day. You can't tell a kid too often that her mommy and daddy love her. Don't you wish you heard it more from your parents? This habit alone can be the difference maker for your family, and I'd love to hear how these ideas have helped you at home.

Asking yourself …

What will I do differently tomorrow?

feeds the Hungers of the Heart by developing the habit of …

Balance

What Will I Do Differently Tomorrow?

●●●●●●●●●●●●●●●●●●●●●●●●●●●●●●●●●●●

I hand out a card at my seminars that has printed on it all of the Habits of the Heart questions. I know that an awful lot of people who get the card end up putting it in their wallet, tossing it aside, or hanging it up somewhere, but they never take these questions seriously, and as a consequence the principles never take root in their hearts. In order for these principles to live in your heart, in order for you to be the good-hearted professional you were designed to be, you must do some things differently. Every day is a new day, full of opportunities to be a difference maker.

To make a difference you must intellectually understand the change process and you must emotionally embrace it. Think in terms of seven stages of emotion in the change process, and you must understand that your leadership team members will go through all seven at various times and at different speeds.

The first stage of embracing change is the *shock* stage, which starts a ripple effect. "Oh no!" you gasp.

Then almost instinctively you respond with *denial:* "It didn't work then and it won't work now."

The next stage is *frustration:* "Why can't it be the way it was?"

After frustration comes the fourth stage, *acceptance,* but before people can accept "the way it is," they first have to look back and mourn "the way it was." It takes time to make that adjustment. As leaders, you can fall into the trap of thinking that change is or should be linear. You want to put out a memo, create the strategy, and implement it. You can be impatient with emotion, but people need time to accept both the inevitability and the process of change.

The fifth emotional stage is *experimentation.* Once you have accepted change, and only after you have accepted change, then you are ready to experiment and try new ways of doing and thinking about things.

When your experimentation leads to an Aha! experience, you move into the *embracing* stage, where you finally see how the change can work.

....

The seventh and final emotional stage is *integration,* when the change becomes a part of you. The newly integrated situation now becomes the baseline that you will fight to the death to avoid changing!

It's okay to resist change initially. What is not all right is continuing to resist change, because change is inevitable and unrelenting.

Unfortunately, changes do not wait until we have fully processed one change before the next one hits. We'd like to get through all seven emotional stages for one change—before we have to handle the next one— but life just isn't that way. We might still be in denial or frustration with the first change when the second change hits us right between the eyes. We recover from that shock and maybe we're now at the stage of acceptance or experimentation, when BOOM! we're hit with another change.

Change is not an event. It is an ongoing process. If we learn to understand change and emotionally embrace change, we will begin to see change as a natural process of life.

Implement today's change and the changes of tomorrow with caring regard for the emotional needs and sensitivities of people. By now perhaps you're weary of the emotional needs of your team members.

··

But if you fail to combine your systems and process changes with respect for the human component of emotion, your ability to change effectively will be undermined. Change is not a linear process. You must incorporate an allowance for natural human emotional responses in order to implement change effectively.

Violating trust destroys the capacity to create positive change. Often the change itself is not as much of a problem as the way the change is led. If you violate trust, or treat others as second class citizens, or make them feel as though their input or feelings are of no value, you destroy the capacity for positive change.

Real behavior change cannot occur without altering your internal guidance system. Your internal guidance system is your values, your beliefs, your assumptions, the choices you make, how you behave, your habits and your attitudes, all of which direct the way you think and your results. Your internal guidance system is what motivates your actions. A good internal guidance system will take you where you want to go even if there is a lot of change and confusion along the way.

A word of warning: Don't bring up internal guidance system issues that you are not willing to act on. Don't bring up values unless you are prepared to

....

live by them. Don't say, "Let's sit down and discuss our core values," unless you are willing to incorporate the values of your team members. And don't put together a mission statement if you're not willing to walk the talk. Otherwise you will breed greater cynicism, you will spawn greater distrust, and you will do more harm than good.

Leaders Developing Leaders

• •

There are four major reasons why most people don't develop leadership skills and why they never become the kind of leader that we're talking about.

1. They've never had somebody lead them. You can't learn what you've never seen.
2. They've had multiple negative experiences. They've become conditioned by repeated negative experiences. *We think the way we do, because of what we believe to be true.* If all you've had is negative experience, you begin to believe the dark things about yourself. Look at

what you believe. Look at how you think. Is it time to change the way you think?

3.   Some people avoid leadership because of fear. For many, it's the fear of success. You say, "I can cope with my present situation, but if I change, if I show that I'm capable of more, then it will be *expected.*"

4.   Many people don't develop leadership skills because they don't trust the leaders in their organization. Trust is established by consistently meeting each other's expectations over a period of time.

Let's look at the seven stages of the leadership development path.

1.   The *internal* stage, when all of your focus, all of your consciousness, all of your thoughts are directed on yourself. You're the only person you think about. We all start here. Don't you dare think you're above this, because we all begin right here at stage one, focused on ourselves. Stage one is where everything is a struggle. It's a struggle to get up, a struggle to go to work, a struggle to read this book about change. You're

....

not ready to progress until you're willing to look outside of yourself.

2. When you're ready to look outside of yourself, you enter the *role model* stage, when you look to other people to teach you how to better develop. You have not reached where you are today without some role models. Because this second stage often includes mimicking role models, it is sometimes referred to as the "fake it till you make it" stage.

3. The *independence* stage is when you begin to think on your own, independent of your role model. Not that they become unimportant, but you gain the ability to think on your own. Many people think there are only three stages to leadership development, and they go through repeated cycles of the internal, role model, and independence stages, without ever questioning whether there is more.

4. In the *introspection* stage, a leader begins to ask some deep personal questions: What do I believe in? What is important? What matters most? What are my values? Do I live my values? Will my values and beliefs be compromised here at work? Can I walk my talk? Can I live my values

here at work or do I have to put them on hold in order to work here? Can I do that? Where's my art? What's my magic? What am I gifted at? What's my passion? What am I awesome at? Can I passionately practice my magic here or will the cumulative activity of doing things I don't believe in kill my passion? A true leader thinks. A true leader gets very introspective.

5. All those deep questions can be unsettling until you enter the *role recognition* stage. In this stage you begin to get some answers to your questions and those answers begin to come in the form of roles—you begin to plug in to the roles that you have as a leader. Leader is a macro role, and here are seven microroles to being a leader:

- managing processes
- facilitating (helping people work through processes)
- mentoring, coaching, or teaching
- being a peer
- communicating
- motivating others
- listening (seek first to understand, then to be understood)

....

6. Once you recognize the subroles of leadership, the next stage is the *mastery* stage, where the leader builds proficiency in each of the seven subroles. Depending on your personality and previous experience, some of these subroles will be easier than others, but all are important.

7. Finally comes the *mentoring* stage, where you turn around and teach what you know to other people.

Habits of the Heart at Work

• •

Every organization has four primary assets: money and resources, products and services, time, and people. People are the most important and valuable asset because they control and direct all the other assets. The effectiveness of any organization is determined by its people—the way they think, their perspectives, their attitudes, and the experiences that they bring to the workplace. You want to create a climate that bolsters the productivity and the potential of your people. You accomplish your objective when you consider the uniquely human elements of emotion, passion and individuality. You achieve your goals when you begin to implement the Habits of the Heart.

....

Here are a few more suggestions that will enhance the human element in your organization.

1. Catch people doing something right. We too easily fall into the trap of expecting good things but only commenting on the bad things. Find the gold that's out there. For every ounce of gold, you may have to excavate five thousand pounds of dirt. But you're not looking for the dirt. You're looking for the gold!

2. When you catch someone doing something right, praise them in writing as well as orally. When you give written compliments, be very specific. Written praise has lasting value.

3. Be an effective leader by being a balanced person. When you learn to balance the varying roles you play, together they make you an effective leader.

4. Keep developing your people even if you don't see any immediate results. Do it because you care. When a farmer plants a seed, he doesn't see immediate results, but he continues the cultivation process through all the stages until harvest—and then he enjoys the fruit of his labor.

5. Think like the customer. Be externally focused in order to meet your customer's needs. Remember Les Jones of Executive Cab Company. Develop his way of thinking, which is more driven by meeting customer needs than by his own profitability.

6. Remember, there is nothing you have that you didn't get without the willing help of someone else. You can have everything in life you want if you just help enough other people get what they want.

7. The only enduring sense of self-worth is based on who you are, not on what you do. All people have exactly the same value; therefore, give everyone VIP treatment.

8. Failure is an event, not a person. Don't think that there are winners and losers in life. There are winners and there are people who have not yet learned how to win.

9. Happiness is the joy of living. Spread it around.

10. Find a way to make work fun. Having fun at work unleashes the hidden, emotional side of people where creativity is found, where commitment is found, where all of those things are found that really make people apply themselves

one hundred percent. Allow people to be themselves. Make the workplace a place of joy. Let people enjoy their work. Unleash the human spirit and you will be successful in the twenty-first century.

Dead Companies Walking

•••••••••••••••••••••••••••••••••

*The business that makes nothing but money
is a poor kind of business.*

—Henry Ford

In what has become the tightest labor market in
thirty years, employers are waking up to the realization
that keeping their people happy is a critical component
of the company's overall financial performance.
Keeping people happy at work is an easily implemented
solution, because it is about responding to their lifestyle
needs. Is your company ignoring the Seven New Vital
Signs for Corporate Health?

What makes people happy? While the key indicators of employee satisfaction are different with every organization, a few tend to be regularly mentioned in almost every company I've worked with. Research and experience has led us to pinpoint seven new vital signs of employee satisfaction, vital signs that will ultimately be the indicators of lasting corporate health in the new economy.

The central principle guiding these new vital signs is—*Build people first; then they will build a company that lasts.* Look into the mirror of the Seven New Vital Signs of Corporate Health and see how your company stacks up. The seven new vital signs are:

1. Demonstrated employer respect for work/life balance.

A life away from work brings life to your work. Marriott Corporation has found that connection to hold true, and has launched a fathering program to better equip their employees with strategies for succeeding at home. Renewal away from work is like life-giving water, we need it to survive. And single employees need it just as badly as those who are married with children.

Even the military recognizes the need for R&R between battles. What is your level of commitment to

••

renewal? I can guarantee you that habitually denying
yourself enjoyable hobbies and activities away from
work, just to spend more time on the job, has a point of
diminishing returns. Take some time for you. It's
amazing how much more productive your seasons of
intensity will be if you can drink from the reservoir of
rest.

2. Trust building.

Violating trust destroys your capacity to create
positive change. Trust can be earned and maintained by
consistent acts that align with aspired values. Here are
four universally accepted acts of trust:

- Practicing fear-free openness in conversation
- Being committed to understanding each other's
  position
- Demonstrating commitment to emotionally
  support each other
- Demonstrating loyalty to established partners

Recently, one of the leading automakers received
a shipment of seats from a vendor who was experi-
encing a labor strike. When asked who had made the
seats while the union was on strike, the vendor

....

explained that replacement workers had been brought in. Having union workers as partners, the automaker refused to use those seats in their vehicles, thereby demonstrating loyalty to the positions of their established partners. Trust is everything.

3. Senior leadership modeling core values.

In the 1950s, two psychologists named Singer and Schacter reported what was at that time a groundbreaking piece of research. They were able to prove that people took their emotional cues for behavior from the culture or environment they were a part of. *Conformance to norms and acceptance by others is a powerful hidden motivator of human beings.* What environment are you unconsciously conforming to?

What kind of operational decision making have you observed in the company you work for? Do the values in your decisions model those core values hanging in the lobby as part of the company's vision statement? For a company's core values to be more than fantasy, people need to see living examples of excellence in leaders. How well does your company model core values? Management must understand that people are watching every move of the leaders and taking their cue from them.

....

4. Employees first, customers second, shareholders third.

When asked, "What is the purpose of business?" most corporate executives say, "To make money." WRONG! If the purpose of business was just making money then your role models would be people whose business makes the most money. But the last time I looked, *The Wall Street Journal* and *Fortune* magazine weren't writing articles about the marketing strategies of crack dealers and drug cartels. I mean after all, their revenues are tax-free.

The purpose of business is more than making money. The purpose of business is to make money *honorably*. Making money honorably takes a different breed of culture where employees are first, customers are second, and shareholders are third.

I was speaking to a Fortune 500 company that was in the middle of the most recent of several rounds of restructuring. Everyone was told how revenues were down and how the company had to adjust in order to compete. They bought it. A lot of companies were doing it and they believed that what the senior leaders were doing was in the best interest of the company. I had been brought in for a series of events that would serve as morale boosters for those who had survived the cuts.

Two months after my events concluded, the CEO announced that the company was buying a minor-league baseball team for a purchase price in the millions. While this was viewed as a slam dunk marketing opportunity by company officials, the real people on the front lines couldn't understand why the money was there for a baseball team but not there for their co-workers dismissed just six months earlier.

Which commitment is the strongest where you work? Building paper profits quickly? Or building people first so they can build a company that lasts? You can't betray people and expect trust, loyalty and commitment. You can't continue to cut your way to paper profitability. At some point you've got to grow the business. The best way to do that is with a commitment to people first, customers second and shareholders third.

5. Making the workplace a fun place to work.

Fun companies are a place where customers continue to come back because of the enjoyable emotional experience they had during the transaction. If you want a place where customers like to go, build a place where co-workers like to work. People's enthusiasm and enjoyment for work is like a magnet for attracting customers.

....

Fun companies have people who bring fresh new ideas to their work because it's exciting to be there. Every day has a new infectious spirit of adventure with creativity oozing out of every office. These companies encourage their people to experiment with new ways of working. They also lead people to accept each other and to build relationships with each other that allow humanity and wholeness to come to work every day. WOW!

6. Finding common ground through unity.

Diversity has taken on a new meaning in the real world of work. Today, diversity means I'll respect your journey, culture and perspectives and you respect mine. And any barrier weakens the spirit of unity. We may work side by side and we may even be on the same project team, but that doesn't mean the barriers have been eliminated.

Respecting each other's journey helps us recognize each other's unique strengths. Superficial respect and limited knowledge of each other is no longer good enough. Businesses today need people with a sense of community in a place where people can see themselves belonging. Let's build a workplace where we can talk with each other about our deepest feelings and needs and seek to genuinely understand each other. Let's go to work in a place where each other's unique strengths can be used to make a difference every day for the team—that's unity. Unity beats diversity every day.

7. Stimulating change from a changeless foundation.

The most critical of the new vital signs you want to nurture is the ability to preserve core values as changeless, while you endlessly stimulate change to meet marketplace demands. That's a stormy sea to sail on, but it is critical because it provides people with anchors during the storms of change. During dynamic times you need people who can think with clarity and make decisions based on a commitment to core values.

With this base, people can learn to renew themselves professionally and stay in demand, with a current set of skills that are valuable in this new economy.

Performing Company Miracles

Remember, we're living in an age of new loyalty. Many companies have cut their staffs to the bone, then carved the bone. They have unwillingly created a mercenary culture of free agency among their people. Expecting their cost-cutting moves to create

....

momentum, these organizations are instead finding uncooperative cynicism. As a result, loyalty to these companies is dead or dying and in its place we are seeing the rise of a new breed of loyalty — to customers, co-workers, family and self — not to the company. Today's business leaders are finding it harder and harder to rebuild a sense of commitment and trust after betrayal.

And somewhere, deep inside such a company, there exists an executive who is gaining ground as she swims against this current. She believes in the value of the individual and seeks to gain every edge for every member of her team. This overlooked champion of people is hard at work doing all she can to help sustain her people during peak seasons of intensity. She works to meet any need they have, emotionally, personally and professionally. She builds hope instead of fear and she is motivated by one single assumption: *Building people first builds an organization that lasts.*

Those who work with her will walk through fire for her because they have seen how she aggressively protects her people while at the same time leading them to exceed expectations. The workplace phenomenon of islands of trust in a cynical sea happens when one person values other people more than what is natural and customary in their culture. We call these islands of trust Company Miracles.

Company Miracles are the flashpoints that re-ignite the flames of commitment. One person can perform a Company Miracle and start a grass-roots recommitment. One person can make a difference even within a culture that devalues people in daily decisions. If you are caught in such a culture, remember there are many paths to success. My prayer is that you will choose the path that's broad enough for what matters most. If that means you choose to stay, think of yourself as a miracle worker who can make magic happen once the people you work with know you are committed to them no matter what.

I hope *Habits of the Heart* makes that kind of a difference for you.

Listed by Speakers Platform as one of the world's best motivational speakers, Jeff Conley sends corporate and association audiences home on a high with a message that matters.

For booking information call:

The Jeff Conley Corporation
Phone: 972–242–4300
Email: Jeff@jeffconley.com